RMS OLYMPIC

BRIAN HAWLEY

AMBERLEY PUBLISHING

FRONT COVER: White Star's salute to the city of Liverpool. On June 1, 1911, after an overnight trip from Belfast, *Olympic* arrived in her port of registry for a brief visit and open house before continuing on to Southampton and her maiden voyage. This painting shows the brand-new liner from the Wirral side of the Mersey. (Original painting by Robert Lloyd from author's collection.)

BACK COVER: The original painting for the famous post-card view of *Olympic* in Plymouth Harbor by renowned British artist Norman Wilkinson. Wilkinson produced a series of paintings for the smoking rooms of the three White Star sisters – 'Approach to the New World' for *Olympic*, 'Plymouth Harbour' for *Titanic*, and (rumor has it) 'Old Liverpool' for *Britannic*. For decades *Titanic* researchers wondered what Wilkinson's painting for *Titanic* looked like. When Wilkinson's son found his father's sketches for the painting, the harbor view for Titanic's Smoking Room was identical to this famous post-card view of *Olympic*, only without the *Olympic*. *Titanic*'s painting had been in front of us the whole time. (Original painting from the Peter Fleming Collection.)

FRONTISPIECE: New York. (The Mariners' Museum)

First published 2012

Amberley Publishing Plc
The Hill, Stroud
Gloucestershire, GL5 4EP

www.amberley-books.com

Copyright © Brian Hawley, 2012

The right of Brian Hawley to be identified as the Author of this work has been asserted in accordance with the Copyrights, Designs and Patents Act 1988.

ISBN 978 1 4456 0093 2

British Library Cataloguing in Publication Data.
A catalogue record for this book is available from the British Library.

Typeset in 10pt on 13pt Celeste.
Typesetting by Amberley Publishing.
Printed in the UK.

CONTENTS

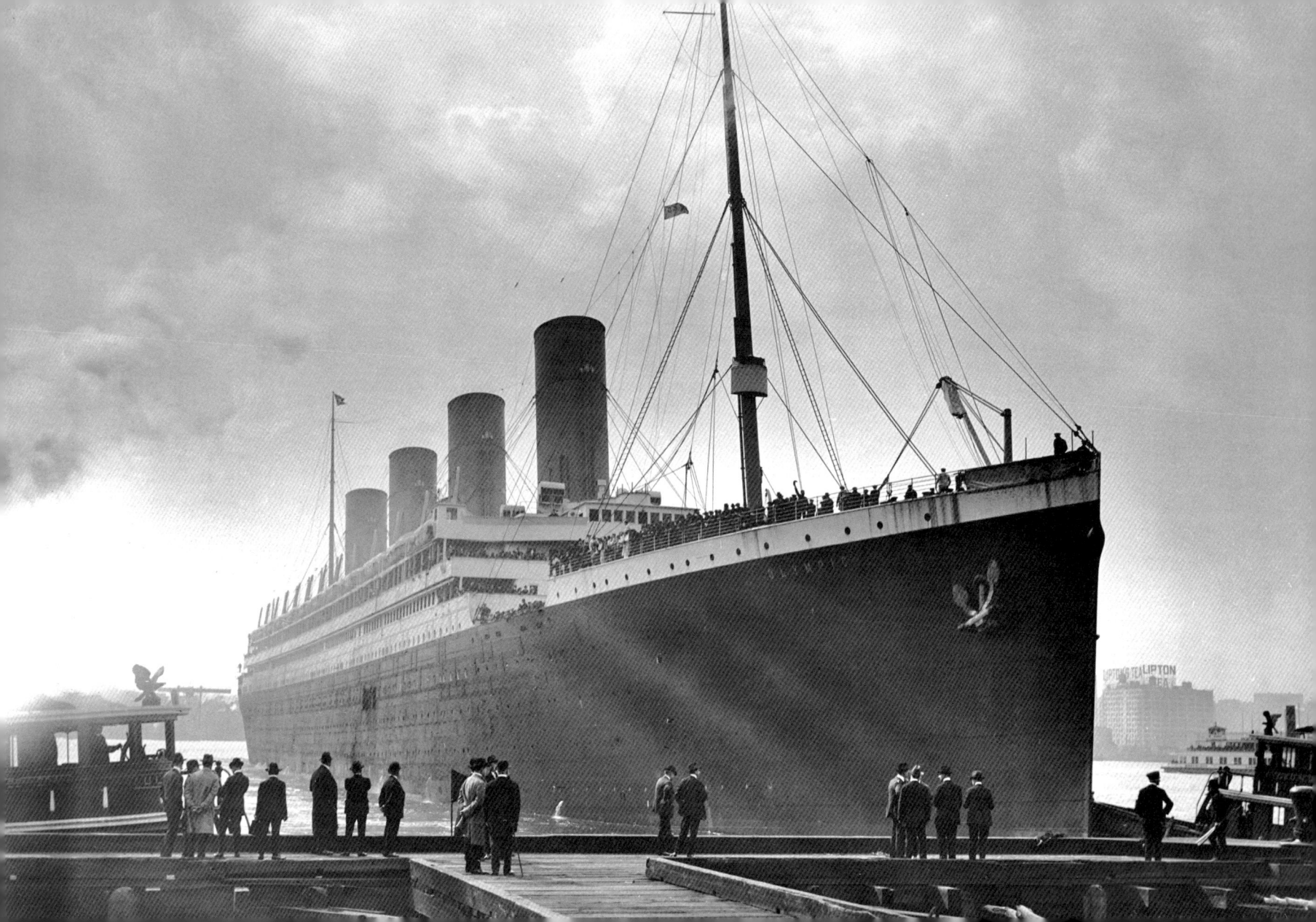

ACKNOWLEDGMENTS

A tremendous number of people very kindly assisted with this book, lending photos, helping with information about the great ship, and providing editorial help. Without their collaboration, this book would not be what it is and could not have been written.

Firstly, a huge thanks to my friend Robert Lloyd, who produced the superb cover art. He is an amazing artist and can bring these old liners to life like few others.

Special thanks to Eric Sauder and Alex Cheek, who helped edit my original notes into a cohesive text and did the final proofing. They improved the book by leaps and bounds.

Thanks to the Titanic International Society (TIS) for lending many rare photos (most of which have never appeared in print), and a special thanks to Catherine Bernstein of TIS for her idea of an iPhone face-time session without which several important photos would not have been included. Thanks also go to the following for lending photos and art: Nelson Arnstein, Rene Bergeron, Peter Boyd-Smith, Stephen Card, Alex Cheek, Peter Davies-Garner, Peter Fleming, Steve Hall, David Hutchings, Ken Marschall, Janette and Campbell McCutcheon, Eric Sauder, Don Stoltenburg, Claes-Göran Wetterholm, John White/White Star Memories, and Braxton Williams.

Ken Marschall deserves a second 'thank you'. The 1912 photo of the first-class staircase in the color section was in terrible condition when I received it. Because of the importance of the picture to maritime researchers, Ken took great pains to improve the image, making it much more presentable, and the final result is stunning.

Museums and archives around the world were searched for many years to complete this book. I owe a debt of gratitude to Claudia Jew at The Mariners' Museum in Newport News, Virginia, for her kind help. Several others were of great assistance, including the Royal Crown Derby Archives, Alastair Arnott of the Southampton Maritime Museum, the ever-helpful Maureen Watry of the Cunard Archives, and Wade Myers at the National Park Service Archive. I would be very remiss if I did not also thank the amazing staff in the curatorial department of Biltmore Estate in Asheville, North Carolina, for their help over the years, including Lori Garst, Leslie Klingner, Laura Overbey, Darren Poupore, and Ellen Rickman. The wartime images of *Olympic* and the sketches of her in dazzle paint came from the National Archives and Records Administration. Michael Trivett at McGee Cad deserves a thank you for carefully scanning the oversized and delicate items from my collection.

Thanks also go to several people who took the time and kindly responded to my question in *Ships Monthly* magazine for information about the tug *Plover*: Robinson Branch, Mr Roger Bye, Ted Carr, Mr A.J. Smythe, and A.S. Walton.

Last but not least are the ocean-liner collectors, researchers, friends, and relatives who helped with this project in ways big and small: Steve Anderson, Mark Baber, Günter Bäbler, David Scott-Beddard, George Behe, the late Frank O. Braynard, Paul Burns, Mike and Sandy Callison, Joe Carvalho, Mike Choi, Ray Cowell, Ralph Currell, Gena and Lewis Elias, Linda Fuller, Charlie Haas, James and Jessie Hawley, Jim and Jane Hawley, Brent Holt, Eric Longo, John Maxtone-Graham, Bill Miller, Patrick Mylon, Mark Nemergut, Mike Poirier, Dave Powers, Una Reilly, Jonathan Smith, Parks Stephenson, Rich Turnwald, Russ Upholster, Jessica and Daniel West, Brandt West, John White, Geoff Whitfield, and Iain Yardley.

I hasten to add, however, that any oversights or errors are mine alone.

INTRODUCTION

On June 14, 1911, the first of the White Star Line's new trio of liners entered service. RMS *Olympic* was an instant triumph with both critics and, much more importantly, the traveling public. Her lovely lines gave a traditional ocean-liner feel; yet at the same time, she was a new apogee in ocean-liner style, one which looked forward to the clean, uncluttered design of the French liner *Normandie* nearly twenty-five years later rather than back to the liners of the nineteenth century. Her builders, Harland & Wolff, were at the peak of their craft during *Olympic*'s construction, and all of their talent and skill went into her. The results were spectacular.

At the time of her debut, the press and the public heaped praise on *Olympic*. She was, by far, the most spacious, well-appointed ship afloat and was filled with new amenities to entertain passengers – reception rooms, a Turkish bath, a swimming pool, a squash court, a gym, an *à la carte* restaurant, to name just a few. Before World War I, only the finest hotels or the private homes of the rich had such luxuries. At sea, they were novel indeed. Maritime historian John Maxtone-Graham observed that the vast amount of space and her clean, yacht-like lines dramatically set her apart from her predecessors and the many ocean liners that

followed. Except for her famous and ill-starred sisters, nothing came close to *Olympic*'s style and elegance in those pre-war years.

Harland & Wolff were justifiably proud of their accomplishment and could point to the amazing feat of having built the two largest liners in the world at the same time side by side. It is almost beyond comprehension to think of the vast quantity of equipment and interior fittings that had to be produced for the two sisters – from their massive boilers to the daintiest of light fixtures. Unlike today's manufacturing companies where outsourcing is the rule, Harland & Wolff produced the vast majority of the items that went into their ships themselves. No delays would have been tolerated by White Star or Harland & Wolff as so frequently plague today's transportation firms.

On May 31, 1911, just two weeks before *Olympic*'s maiden voyage, Harland & Wolff and White Star achieved one of the greatest public-relation successes in transatlantic history. Just after noon, *Titanic* was successfully launched at Belfast's famous Harland & Wolff shipyard. Nearby, gleaming with a fresh coat of paint, the brand-new *Olympic* waited to begin her first voyage to her home port of Southampton. At that moment, White Star had the hottest properties in the transatlantic trade.

Olympic, however, did not head directly for Southampton, the famous port which she would call home. First, she had a special stop to make in Liverpool, her port of registry. The Liverpool call, where she was opened for public viewing, was practically a necessity because of the unusual situation in which White Star found itself in 1911. Four years earlier, the company had moved their main-line ships to Southampton, and the magnificent new *Olympic* was never intended to provide transatlantic service to and from Liverpool despite White Star still being headquartered there. Liverpool's city fathers felt the loss of the large White Star liners to Southampton profoundly; so *Olympic*'s salute to the city was a bittersweet call – one that no one thought she would ever make again.

The weather for *Olympic*'s Liverpool call could not have been better. Thousands of Liverpudlians turned out and paid half-a-crown to tour the behemoth. That night, *Olympic* continued to Southampton where she was again open to public viewing, the proceeds from all such 'open houses' going to local charities. White Star welcomed as many dignitaries and staff on board as possible in the two weeks before the maiden crossing, but perhaps the most important were the line's own agents. These all-important guests had the job of selling the new ship to thousands of prospective passengers.

As White Star's press department intended, coverage of the new liner had been near constant since she was laid down in 1908; however, much of that was concentrated in the nautical trade journals. Now that she was ready to carry passengers, newspaper and magazine coverage in the United Kingdom and the United States boomed. There was palpable excitement running through the press and the transatlantic trade in anticipation of *Olympic*. She achieved great success on her maiden voyage, amply meeting, even exceeding, all the goals her owners and builders had set for her. White Star's understandable pride was summed up with this simple quote by J. Bruce Ismay at the end of the maiden voyage: 'The *Olympic* is a marvel and has given unbounded satisfaction.'

When the newest liner on the Atlantic made her debut in Manhattan, dozens of newspapermen were on the dock to meet her. Like today's celebrity fascination, social news sold papers in 1911 and immediately cemented *Olympic*'s spot as a favorite on the Atlantic, especially among the wealthy. The famous flocked to her early on, one of the first being Mrs. William K. Vanderbilt, Jr, who traveled on the return maiden voyage 'incognito', fleeing to Europe to escape her failing marriage. Being one of the celebrities of the day, she could hardly have traveled without it making the papers, especially on the largest ship in the world, even under an assumed name.

At the time of her entry into service, *Olympic* was hailed as a floating palace. Like most things in life, that simplified description was accurate enough, but the reality was more nuanced. She was a ship of many firsts: A reception room, a proper pool (not a plunge bath), an elevator for second-class passengers, a squash court. As the size of liners increased, more space could be allocated to such amenities.

White Star, like all steamship companies, wanted to build the best ship they could without spending too much money. After all, the trio was built with borrowed funds and had to be paid back. Cunard faced the same problem and fared much worse with this same return-on-investment concern when constructing *Mauretania* in 1907. Her builders, Swan Hunter, came in way over budget, which made it very difficult, even with her government subsidy, for *Mauretania* to make enough to pay off her building costs and contribute to building a future replacement. This disastrous situation meant that *Mauretania* cost hundreds of thousands of pounds more than her sister *Lusitania*, and Cunard was furious at the cost overruns. White Star needed the final cost of *Olympic* to be around £1,500,000, and given their harmonious and lengthy relationship with Harland & Wolff, this was achieved.

For their money, White Star received the best possible value of any pre-war ship *Olympic* could be compared to. Unlike the German *Imperator*, which had severe stability issues, *Olympic* was known as a very good sea boat, prone to less movement in the rough conditions of the North Atlantic. Taste is subjective, but many find that *Olympic* was the most beautiful of the liners built before World War I. She had grace and bore none of the ponderousness of *Imperator* or the quirkiness of *Aquitania*. *Olympic* represented White Star's highest achievement. Spacious, luxurious, economical, and relatively inexpensive to build, she was fast enough to be competitive and very popular – a ship owner's dream and a shipbuilder's pride. When completed, she was the largest ship in the world, a title she gained again a second time after the loss of her slightly larger sister *Titanic*.

Olympic was so innovative that rival shipping companies sent spies on board to critique the liner and her amenities then report back to their headquarters. Cunard, for example, rushed to incorporate some of her best features into the new *Aquitania* then under construction. Perhaps the area where White Star achieved the best results was in *Olympic*'s layout. She was a ship built with the future in mind, and her designers' helpful forethought served *Olympic* well once the easy-money days of pre-war immigration were over. It is telling that little in the way of real renovations were required in her accommodation until the later part of the 1920s. This flexible design meant that throughout much of her post-war career *Olympic* was consistently more profitable than her fleet mates *Majestic* and *Homeric*. When she returned to service in 1920, White Star's president, Harold Sanderson, in a biblical reference, called her their 'one ewe lamb'. That she was White Star's prized possession was never in doubt. Sir William Robertson quipped that *Olympic* might have also been called their 'one ewe ram'.

One of the biggest attractions for her wealthiest passengers was the huge variety of large and spacious suites, which were the largest and best appointed in the world in 1911. They shone particularly well when matched against the rather spartan suites on board *Aquitania*. *Olympic* also represented a huge step forward in the number of private baths attached to first-class cabins. Another draw to prospective passengers was the prestige that came with sailing on the newest and largest liner in the world. She was *the* ship on which to see and be seen. Royalty, movie stars, millionaires galore all sailed on her. Many hopeful mothers with daughters of marrying-age also chose to sail on her solely because of her passenger list, which frequently read like a *Who's Who*. After all, what could be better for a young, unmarried girl than to have a deck chair next to the heir to a British fortune? Oddly, numerous survivors of her ill-fated sister *Titanic* sailed on her as well. One has to wonder what possessed them to do so after the horrors they had witnessed on her nearly identical twin.

Olympic's completion signaled the start of a brief period that saw White Star at the pinnacle of its ascent, which ended on April 15, 1912, after the tragedy that befell *Titanic*. White Star would never again reach such a high point. After the loss of *Titanic*, bad news seemed to dog the company, and much of this trouble was far outside the company's control – the outbreak of World War I, the almost inevitable bankruptcy of parent company International Mercantile Marine (IMM) in 1915, the sinking of *Britannic* in 1916, and the multiple failed attempts by a weakened IMM to sell White Star following the war. Perhaps the biggest blow to White Star and all other transatlantic passenger shipping in the 1920s came from the drastically reduced immigration to the United States because of new quotas. Starting in 1921 with the Emergency Quota Act and more significantly under the 1924 Johnson–Reed Act, immigration to the United States, which had been running at more than one million per year, was radically cut back to 150,000 a year once fully implemented.

Shortly thereafter, the disastrous sale of White Star to Royal Mail in 1927 resulted in huge amounts of debt, compounded by exceedingly poor management that led to the rot that eventually hollowed out the company. One can speculate that perhaps a more successful management team would have surmounted all the obstacles White Star encountered in the 1920s, including the inability to finance new ships and the huge inflation in post-war shipbuilding costs.

The disastrous Royal Mail merger also sank the careers of many lifetime White Star officers. As is typical with all mergers, one company comes out firmly on top, and Royal Mail's people were given seniority and the choicest commands which, of course, included *Olympic*. The career track of any successful officer, that long and slow plodding climb up the ladder, resulted in becoming Commodore of the fleet if you lived long enough or were lucky enough. This position of power often brought a knighthood and was the goal of all good officers who might, however briefly, fly their pennant before mandatory retirement forced them out at age 62. This decades-long process of advancement was derailed for White Star's long-serving officers in 1927 because Royal Mail promoted their own over White Star's. For example, Royal Mail's Captain Parker went from the *Albertic* of 18,000 tons to *Homeric* and then to the 46,000-ton *Olympic*, all within a year, neatly skipping over many deserving and long-waiting White Star officers.

The last nail in White Star's coffin was the sweeping Depression that began in 1930. Atlantic traffic plummeted, and all the big lines and liners suffered, *Olympic* being no exception. The huge drop in passenger numbers punished the already-suffering Royal Mail Line mercilessly, and they went bankrupt in 1930, dragging White Star down with it. The chairman, Lord Kylsant, went to prison for cooking the books, and White Star and *Olympic*, caught up in these events, limped along under the control of the British government with most bills being deferred by the Exchequer in a desperate jobs program, the government hardly knowing what to do with this huge, famous, and failing company. There was a real

chance that White Star would be liquidated if a buyer couldn't be found.

For *Olympic*, her fate was sealed during the lengthy and complicated behind-the-scenes negotiations that led to Cunard and White Star merging in 1934. Within a few months of first hoisting the double house flag of the new Cunard White Star Line, *Olympic* was laid up. Her subsequent scrapping was, as one White Star officer put it, because of Cunard management's bias toward their own ships. It has been said that the only thing wrong with *Olympic* was the color of her funnels. One has to wonder how different things would have been had all three *Olympic*-class sisters survived and sailed successfully for White Star into the 1930s.

As with many of the great liners scrapped during the depths of the Depression, *Olympic* was recycled with, what is to modern eyes, amazing thoroughness. Anything that could be stripped off these ships was bought and put to further use, even mundane items like acres of pine decking, linoleum floor tiles, urinals, and bathroom stalls. Entire public rooms were removed and reused, including the first-class Lounge, now famously living on at the White Swan Hotel in Alnwick, England, which prompted the author to make a pilgrimage to see the room in 2010.

Today, pieces of *Olympic* are highly prized among ocean-liner collectors. Large on-board fittings like carved woodwork, paneling, light fixtures, furniture, down to smaller pieces such as china and silver and gift-shop souvenirs are all vacuumed up by voracious collectors. There seems to be no end to the lengths collectors will go to obtain a piece of this beloved ship.

Celebrity Cruises added the glory of *Olympic* to one of its own ships in the year 2000, outfitting a restaurant on board the *Millennium* with the elaborately carved and gilded French walnut panelling from *Olympic*'s famous *à la carte* Restaurant, prompting liner buffs to book a trip on the *Millennium* specifically to have diner in those historic surroundings. What a great tribute to *Olympic*, not to mention a great marketing opportunity for Celebrity, as that restaurant belongs at sea.

Olympic's story is one of joy and great memories for those who traveled in her. She was a trendsetter and, perhaps in the best form of flattery, was heavily copied by the competition. *Olympic* was White Star's 'Ship Magnificent' – dependable and profitable just when the company needed it most. That her admirable service life was overshadowed by other sad events was no reflection on her popularity or her performance. Her traits shone through all the trials and world events she endured, and she remained popular to the end.

Some ships seem to have 'it', that special, undefinable something that sets a liner apart. Cunard's *Queen Mary* and *Mauretania* of 1907, the French Line's *Normandie*, and Holland America's *Rotterdam* of 1959 – all had something that made them special. 'It' is often described by passengers and crew as a soul or a feeling or the sense of camaraderie on board. Whatever 'it' was, *Olympic* had it in abundance.

She was a ship born in the Edwardian era, which served steadfastly in war, shone brightly throughout the Roaring 20s, and met her fate amidst the growing darkness of the Depression and the gathering war clouds over Europe.

She really was the 'Old Reliable'.

Brian Hawley,
At sea on board *Queen Mary 2*, May, 2011.

CHAPTER 1

BUILDING A GIANT

Left: From the early stages of design, spaciousness was a hallmark of the *Olympic*-class vessels. Taken while the liner was still on the stocks, this view, looking aft along the starboard Boat Deck next to the officers' quarters, seems like an exaggerated artist's rendering sometimes used to make ships in period advertising look larger than they were.

According to *The New York Times*, by early March, 1910, several of the principal decks had already been plated, and the partitions and houses on some of the decks had been installed. They also noted that the engine and boiler casings were well advanced. The entrance to the officers' quarters can be seen in the center of the photo between the last two wooden braces. At this stage during construction, the officers' quarters was bolted together, not riveted. (The Mariners' Museum)

Right: Unlike most ships then and now, *Olympic* was lovely from almost any angle. The graceful curve of her steel hull plates merging under her counter accentuates her lines. The dark hull to the right of *Olympic* is, of course, her younger sister *Titanic*. Both ships were built under the famous Arrol Gantry designed for Harland & Wolff by the Scottish engineer William Arrol, whose other projects included the Tower Bridge in London and the Forth Bridge in Edinburgh. (The Mariners' Museum)

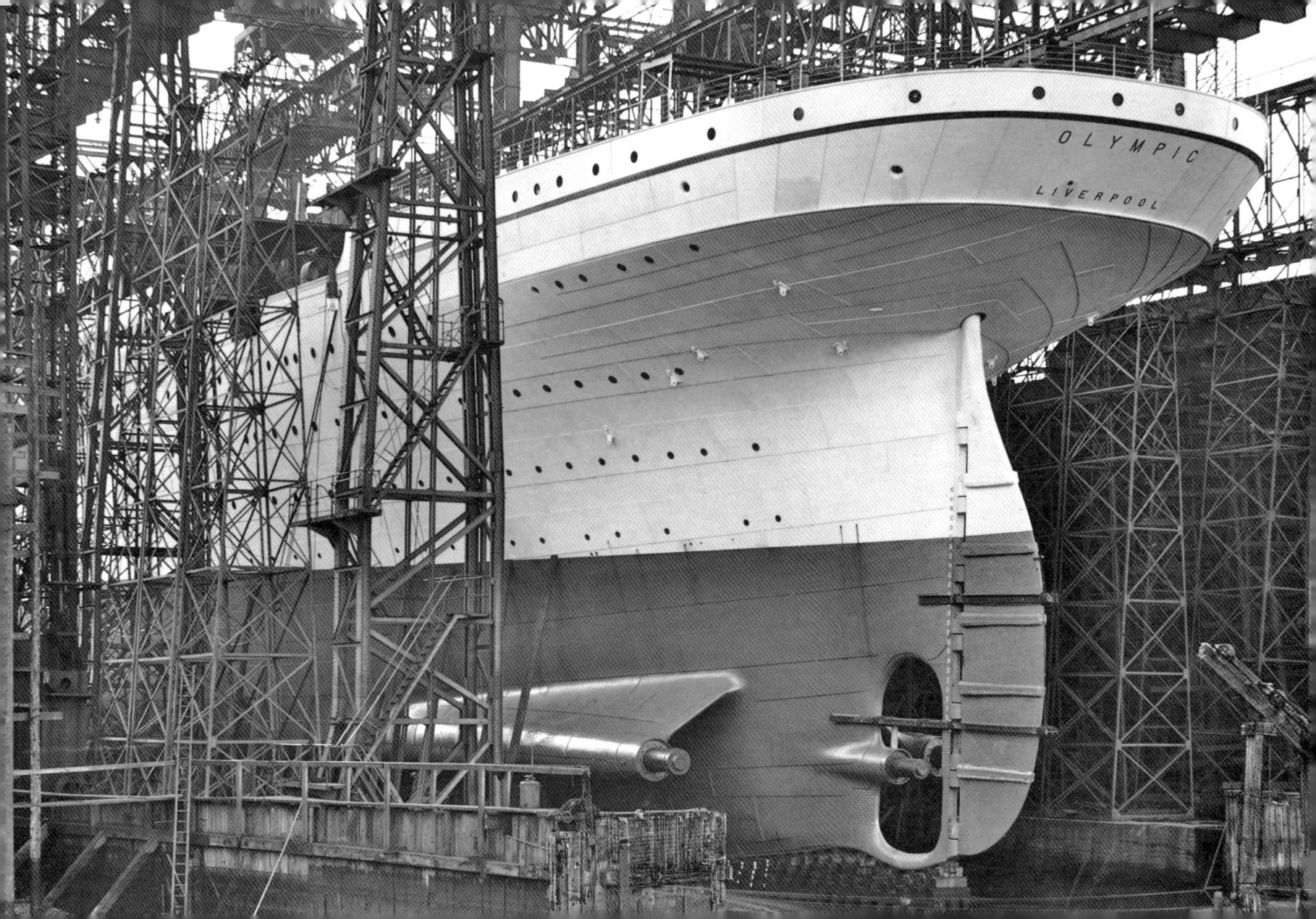

Left: The triple-screw concept of two reciprocating engines – each driving a single wing propeller – and a center low-pressure turbine driving a center screw was extremely successful. Not only was *Olympic* cheaper to build than most of the other large liners on the transatlantic service, but she also still had a great service speed and was much more economical to run when compared to her all-turbine competition. It is curious that the other major transatlantic lines never copied the reciprocating/turbine design. (The Mariners' Museum)

Above: October 20, 1910, at 11 a.m. The weather on launch day was ideal, with bright sunshine after a night of rain. From the white-and-crimson-draped stand, the VIPs watched as the launch triggers were released and Hull 400 began her first journey. Within 62 seconds she was waterborne, having reached a maximum speed of 12½ knots.

White Star went to great expense to paint *Olympic* white before launch to accentuate her lines and show off her hull. White Star and Harland & Wolff knew that dozens of press reporters and photographers would be present for the momentous occasion and wanted the ship to look her best. Because she was never painted white for cruising in the 1930s (unlike her Cunard rival *Mauretania*), photos of her launch give a good idea of how beautiful she looked in this lighter livery. (LuxuryLinerRow.com)

After launch, *Olympic* was towed to the fitting-out basin where thousands of workers installed her interior fittings and machinery. At this stage, the vessel is far from complete, and she is only a shell; thus she is riding very high out of the water. (The Mariners' Museum)

Left: The floating German crane lifting one of the boilers into the ship. The engine arrangement and 29 boilers on board *Olympic* were her hidden strengths. Compared to HAPAG's *Imperator* or Cunard's *Aquitania*, *Olympic* was unbelievably economical to run. *Olympic* could average about 22 knots, nearly the same service speed as her two rivals, on far less coal – 1,080 tons per day for *Imperator* and 950 for *Aquitania* versus 650 for *Olympic*. White Star must have loved seeing *Olympic* sail into port just a scant few hours after her fuel-hungry rivals. (Peter Davies-Garner Collection)

Right: Fitting out is rapidly progressing on the starboard Boat Deck looking forward. On the left, the raised roof of the first-class Smoking Room can be seen. Note the piles of pine decking, each plank being about 3 inches thick. During fitting-out, ships are beehives of activity. 1912 was very much a time when things were made by hand with very little outsourcing or prefabrication; so Harland & Wolff employed nearly 14,000 men at the time *Olympic* was built. (Peter Davies-Garner Collection)

Receiving her first coat of in-service colors. Unlike many other shipbuilding yards (John Brown, for example), Harland & Wolff did not make it a practice to fit the propellers on their ships before launch. They were installed many months later when the vessel was dry docked for the first time. *Olympic*'s propellers can be seen, disassembled, sitting on the dock at the lower right. Her two wing propellers each had a diameter of 23½ feet. The Thompson Graving Dock is located in the foreground and is full of water, ready to receive the liner. She is already the world's largest moving object and soon will be the most luxurious ship in the world. (Peter Davies-Garner Collection)

Right: Steam pours from the temporary boilers installed on *Olympic*'s forward well deck to give power to the capstans so the ship could be warped into dry dock. The operations to maneuver the liner into the dock began at 10 a.m. and were completed by the tugs *Hercules* and *Jackal* within an hour and a half.

At the time *Olympic* and *Titanic* were built, the Thompson Graving Dock was the largest dry dock in the world and the only one capable of holding them, and even then just barely. The door to the dock has a special '*Olympic* and *Titanic* setting' to give those much needed extra few feet for these two massive liners. It holds over 20,000,000 gallons and could be emptied in an amazing 100 minutes. It was officially opened on April 1, 1911, and *Olympic* was the first ship to enter it. (Peter Davies-Garner Collection)

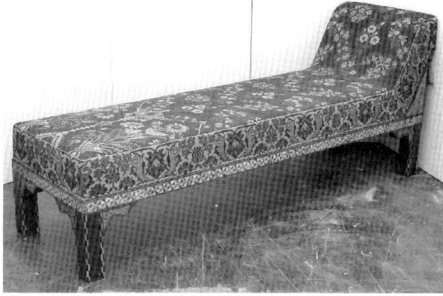

Above: A chaise lounge from the cooling room of *Olympic*'s Turkish Bath. Inlaid with mother of pearl, this is the only fixture from the Turkish Bath that has been found. (Alex Cheek Collection)

Right: All the major shipbuilding yards that constructed ocean liners in the United Kingdom early last century had special facilities to produce mock-ups of the various public rooms to show the client how the spaces would appear when complete although only small sections of the rooms were built. This rare image shows part of *Olympic*'s Turkish Bath Cooling Room, including the beautiful blue and green wall tiles made famous by their discovery intact and in situ in the wreck of *Titanic*. (*Titanic* International Society, Joe Carvalho Collection)

Left: *Olympic*'s massive hull sits in the Thompson Graving dock for the first time and is ready to receive her propellers. All the dots in the light painted area at the water line are individual drain openings for urinals, sinks, bathtubs, etc. As the amount of plumbing on the ship increased, the number of these holes continued to rise. By the time *Britannic*, the third of the trio, was built, she was fitted with a central sewage plant. A similar facility was later installed on *Olympic*. (Peter Davies-Garner Collection)

Left: The port aft corner of the first-class Reception Room while still under construction, showing the shadows of the double portholes behind the arched leaded-glass window. Between each set of portholes and the leaded glass, a pane of milky diffusion glass was installed to help diffuse the light. Here it is either lowered out of sight or has not been installed yet. Of the pair of portholes, only the upper, smaller one opened. The Dining Room is just through the pair of arched windows on the left. Because this room flooded so slowly on *Titanic*, most of these lovely leaded-glass windows and other fittings are still intact on the wreck. (*Titanic* International Society, Joe Carvalho Collection)

Above: Olympic's basin trials were run on May 2, and the engines, having been disconnected from the propellers, ran to everyone's satisfaction. On May 25, she was registered in Liverpoool and given her official number, 131346, and her call letters, MKC. Her two-day sea trials began in Belfast Lough on May 29 with only 250 essential personnel on board. Unlike the Cunard flyers *Lusitania* and *Mauretania*, however, *Olympic* was not put through a strenuous series of runs on the measured mile. Significantly, though, her rudder and turning capabilities were tested several times at full speed with the helm hard over as well as with one engine in reverse. These tests would take on added significance for her sister less than one year later in the middle of the Atlantic. (Steve Hall Collection)

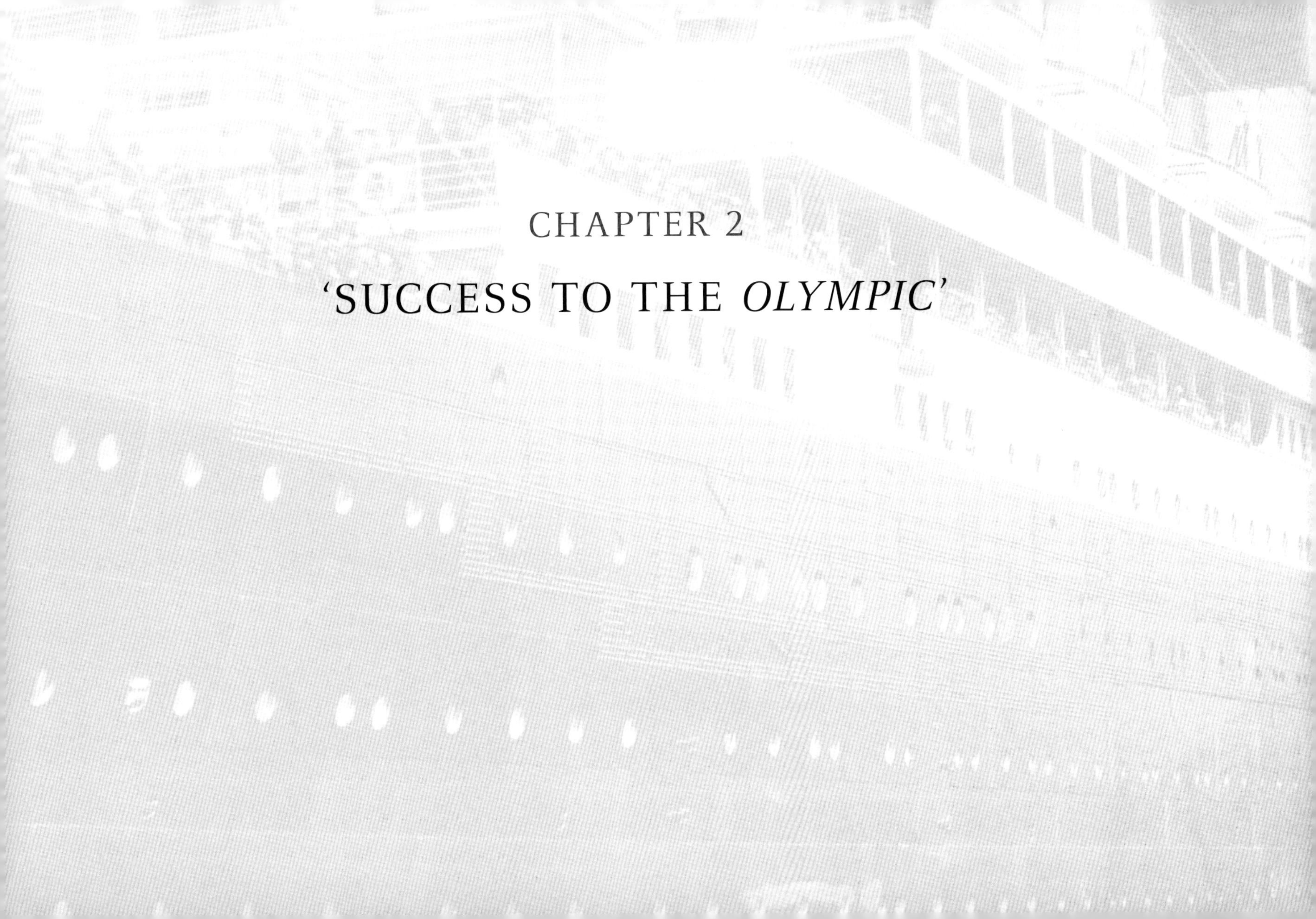

CHAPTER 2

‘SUCCESS TO THE *OLYMPIC*’

Above left: June 1, 1911. What more could White Star have asked for? It was a warm, sunny day in Liverpool, perfect weather to show off their new liner. She was open to the public for a shilling per head and made a great impression on the thousands of people who toured her. All the profits went to local charities. This view was taken from the clock tower on the famous Royal Liver Building and looks directly over the top of the landing stage. (LuxuryLinerRow.com)

Left: Early in her career, *Olympic*'s bridge wings were flush with the side of the ship. Following a suggestion believed to have been made by Captain Smith to give the officers better ability to see when docking or maneuvering, her bridge wings and those of her sister *Titanic* were extended over the ships' sides.

Also visible is the hole for her emergency bow anchor. In practice, shipping this 16-ton anchor would have been difficult even in the best of circumstances, let alone an emergency. To do so required the use of the crane on the forecastle at the extreme bow. Despite its apparent uselessness, carrying this center anchor was required by the Board of Trade. (LuxuryLinerRow.com)

Above right: *Olympic*'s visit to Liverpool followed the high-water mark of White Star's history. Just the day before, *Titanic* was launched and the completed *Olympic* left Harland & Wolff. White Star was justifiably proud. After a successful day in her port of registry, she sailed from Liverpool at 11:15 p.m. for Southampton. (LuxuryLinerRow.com)

An amazing pre-maiden voyage photo of *Olympic* berthed in the White Star Dock in Southampton shortly after her early morning arrival from Liverpool on June 3. Because she will shortly begin taking on the 4,000 tons of coal needed for her first voyage to New York, she has been warped too far out from the pier to use the regular passenger gangways; so a temporary gangway stretching to the D-Deck entrance has been put in place. Coaling was a very dusty business, and the process had to be completed long before passengers embarked so all interior spaces could be cleaned. Less than a year later, a view of her vast expanse similar to this was seen by some of *Titanic*'s passengers from their lifeboats as they left the doomed liner. (Claes-Göran Wetterholm Collection)

White Star had tremendous labor troubles that only worsened from 1911 on. The company had to deal with strikes by stewards, stokers, porters, stevedores, and even coalers. In order to get enough fuel into *Olympic* for the maiden voyage, White Star had to bring in strike breakers from as far as the Continent. There could be no delays, and the ship had to sail on her maiden voyage on time.

In the period before World War I, liners were quite profitable. Emigration helped smooth out the edges of packed high-season sailings compared to the scant bookings of the low season. Third class westbound was often full year-round. After the war, ship owners often looked back to the time before the Great War as a golden age for liners. It was sometimes very difficult to make the ships pay in the 1920s and 1930s with new immigration quotas in place. (J&C McCutcheon Collection)

Arriving in New York Harbor after the completion of a highly anticipated maiden voyage, *Olympic* had made the crossing in 5 days, 16 hours, and 42 minutes at a speed of 21.7 knots. She burned 3,540 tons of coal. During her layover in New York, the great liner was thrown open to the public as she had been in Belfast, Liverpool, and Southampton. Over 16,000 people visited her in New York, paying a total of more than $2,000 for distribution to local charities.

On the lighter side, *The New York Times* reported: 'Her 750 cabin passengers had not left the ship two hours on Thursday when notice came from the White Star office that 1,000 members of the American Engineers' Society would visit the *Olympic* at 2 p.m. What Purser McElroy, known familiarly as 'the Eastern Despot', and Chief Steward Latimer said when they heard this news was improper, and what Chief Engineer Fleming, who had got all his staff busy below overhauling gear, said was unthinkable.'

When *Olympic* departed New York for her return maiden voyage on June 28, 1911, she set a record by carrying the most passengers ever on one ship, 2,301 in first, second, and third class. *The New York Times* reported that she carried 60 maids and valets. (Peter Davies-Garner Collection)

Above: Launched in 1891, HMS *Hawke* was an Edgar-class protected cruiser. She is best known for her collision on September 20, 1911, with White Star's *Olympic*. *Olympic* had sailed from Southampton just after 11 a.m. for her fifth round trip to New York. As she made her way down Southampton Water, just past the Bramble off the Isle of Wight, the *Hawke* began to overtake the liner. Because of the suction created by *Olympic* moving through the water, the *Hawke* was pulled into her and struck her starboard stern quarter. According to *Olympic*'s log, the collision occurred at 12:46 in the afternoon in clear, fine weather. An inquiry was held following the accident, which determined that the collision was caused solely by faulty navigation on the part of *Olympic*'s pilot. The court ruled that the two ships were considered 'crossing vessels', meaning that the *Hawke* had the right of way and that *Olympic* should have given her a wider berth.

Just over three years later, on October 15, 1914, the *Hawke* was torpedoed and sunk with the loss of most of her crew by the German submarine *U-9* and became the fourth British cruiser sunk by this U-Boat in a month. (Brian Hawley Collection)

Opposite: After being holed both above and below the waterline – the lower hole being made by the *Hawke*'s antiquated ram – *Olympic* settled slightly at the stern. The collision opened up second- and third-class cabins on E and F decks. Fortunately, the cabins were empty at the time of the collision because passengers were having lunch. Two compartments were flooded, and according to testimony at the inquiry held to look into the cause of the collision, she took on about 400 tons of water as a result of the damage. 400 tons of anything sounds like a lot, but given the great size of *Olympic*, this was a very small amount, given that she usually carried 5,000 tons of coal.

As expected on a high-season crossing, *Olympic* was supposed to be nearly at capacity for the trip. First class was bursting with nearly 30 American millionaires and notables including Robert Taft, the president's son; Waldorf Astor; and Mr and Mrs Harry Payne Whitney. Despite her famous passengers being anxious to get to New York, the damage was too severe and the crossing had to be canceled. As all the passengers had contracts with White Star to get them to New York, they were 'guests' of the company until alternative passage could be found. Given that nearly all other ships on the Atlantic were also sailing full, finding space on other liners for *Olympic*'s inconvenienced passengers took some doing. (Ken Marschall Collection)

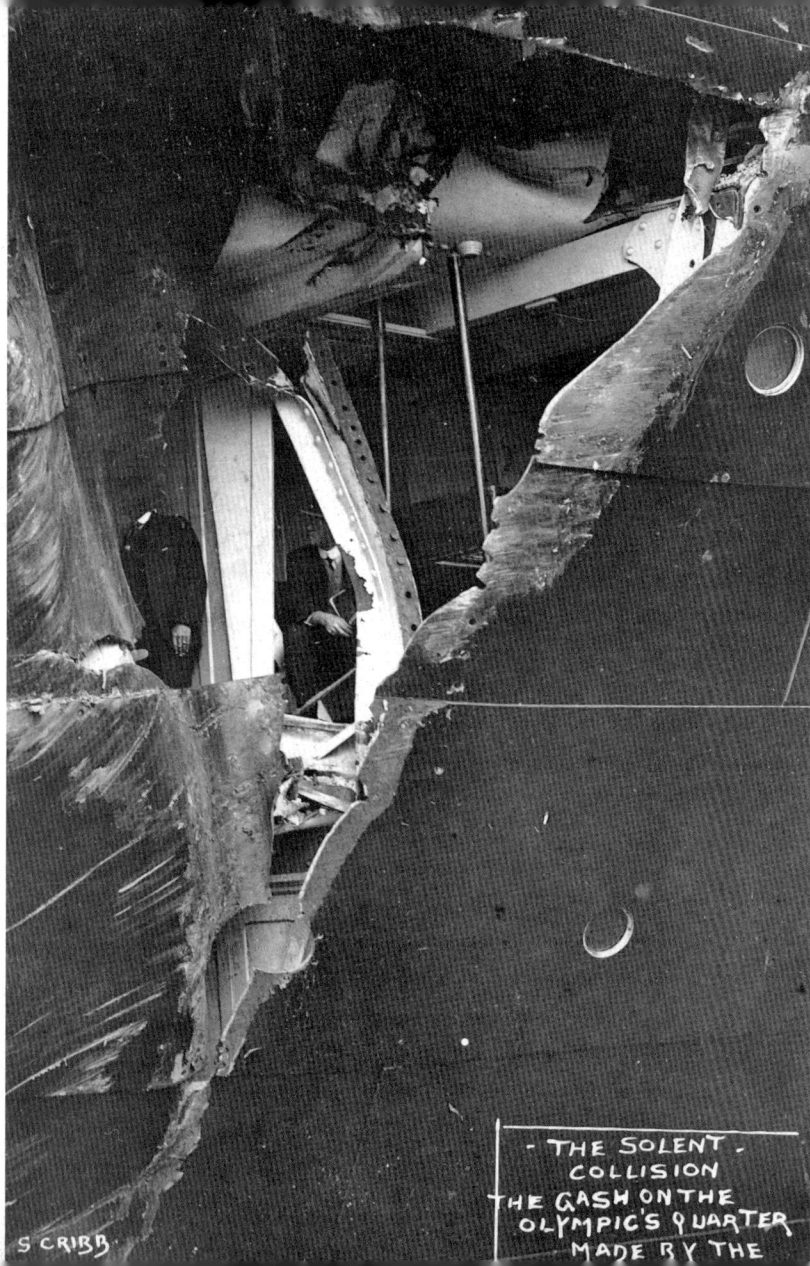

THE SOLENT.
COLLISION
THE GASH ON THE
OLYMPIC'S QUARTER
MADE BY THE

S CRIBB

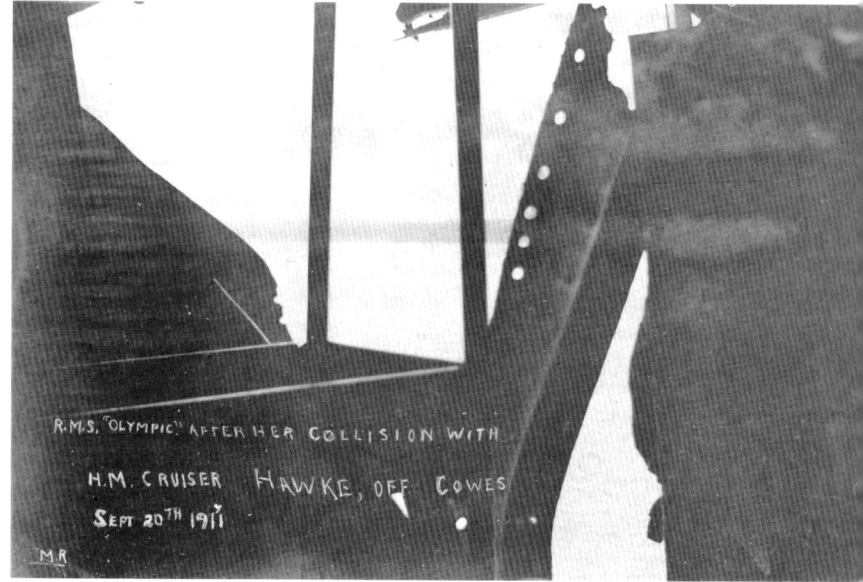

R.M.S. "OLYMPIC" AFTER HER COLLISION WITH
H.M. CRUISER HAWKE, OFF COWES
SEPT 20TH 1911

M.R

Left: Two men, perhaps maritime surveyors, examine the damage to *Olympic* after her collision with the *Hawke*. The accident made great fodder for the press with the world's largest and safest ship having survived a 'devastating' collision. *The New York Times* reported that Captain Smith, not knowing the extent of the damage to the ship, chose to anchor her in Cowes Roads near a mud bank should she need to be beached. The paper continued that women 'screamed and cried as lifeboats and lifebelts were readied' but that the male passengers, 'being generally men of affairs and not easily exercised', were of great help to the crew. (LuxuryLinerRow.com)

PHOTO-ENG · DIVERS REPAIRING THE OLYMPIC AFTER COLLISION WITH HMS HAWKE

Opposite right: A unusual perspective of the damage to *Olympic* from inside the ship, looking out through a bank of former second-class cabins. Because of the massive damage to her flank, *Olympic* had to return to Belfast, where she arrived on October 5 after temporary repairs in Southampton to make her seaworthy for the voyage. She returned to regular service on November 29, having missed three round trips. (LuxuryLinerRow.com)

Top: Divers at work examining the underwater damage. Diving in 1911 was in its infancy; so there was a lack of knowledge of the bends and other diving-related issues. Many of the technical aspects of diving were finally resolved thirty years later by the US Navy during World War II. Commercial diving was, as it is today, highly specialized work made all the more difficult in 1911 by the primitive equipment. (LuxuryLinerRow. com)

Bottom: *Olympic* back at Harland & Wolff early in her career, perhaps for repairs from the *Hawke* collision or her dropped propeller blade in February, 1912. Harland & Wolff had the only dry dock in the world large enough to accommodate the liner, which forced her to return to the builder's yard for needed repairs. This costly and time-consuming issue with drydock space was finally addressed in 1913 as Southampton upgraded its own drydock facilities. (Peter Boyd-Smith Collection)

Olympic's first voyage after the *Titanic* disaster. Even though White Star had put enough additional collapsible boats on board to ensure there was a lifeboat seat for every man, woman, and child aboard, dozens of her crew deserted because of their heightened concern about the safety of the newly loaded collapsibles, meaning that there was not enough crew to work the boilers. A passenger, the Duke of Sutherland, attempted to raise a crew of volunteer yachtsmen to man the stokeholds as far as Queenstown, where it was thought that a new crew of stokers could be raised. White Star, of course, politely declined the offer and was forced to cancel the voyage. She is seen here at anchor on April 28, 1912. (J&C McCutcheon Collection)

This view taken during a summer sailing in 1913 looks aft down the starboard Boat Deck and shows double-stacked and nested lifeboats on the left filling virtually every available space. White Star had an understandable preoccupation with lifeboats after the *Titanic* disaster, and they spent a fortune refitting *Olympic* with enough boats for all. All these additional boats wreaked havoc on *Olympic*'s Boat Deck, as they did on many other liners. For the rest of *Olympic*'s service life, the boat configurations were changed over and over again. Equipment was replaced; tackle and gear improved. Her sister *Britannic* saw even more money spent on boats and equipment in an attempt to unclutter the first-class section of her Boat Deck. Sadly, wartime demands derailed Harland & Wolff's best-laid plans, and *Britannic* sailed as a hybrid, using newly designed gantry davits and filling in with the older-style Welin Quadrant. (Peter Boyd-Smith Collection)

Some of the modifications that took place after the loss of *Titanic* are quite evident in this 1913 view. The slatted boxes in front of the lifeboats held ropes used in lowering the boats and were placed on *Britannic* as well. Fortunately, post-war changes to *Olympic*'s lifeboat configuration resulted in more deck space. This view of the starboard Boat Deck was taken looking forward, and the stairs to the raised roof of the first-class Lounge are visible in the foreground. The sliding weather door on the left accesses a small staircase which led down to the first-class A Deck Promenade. (Peter Boyd-Smith Collection)

Despite her massive size, *Olympic* was subject to the whims of the weather just like any smaller liner. On January 18, 1912, *The New York Times* reported about the worst of a massive storm *Olympic* suffered through on January 4. En route from Southampton to New York, *Olympic*, with Captain E.J. Smith in command, shipped a huge wave that tore off the eighteen-square-foot, four-ton cover on her No. 1 hatch. The wave carried the hatch cover over the rail at the aft end of the forecastle and deposited it on the well deck below. The heavy sea also broke a porthole in the cabin of White Star's managing director J. Bruce Ismay, who told reporters in New York that, despite her size and the fact that the ship rolled and pitched a great deal, her promenade deck remained dry and a majority of her passengers were able to make it to the saloon for their meals. (Peter Boyd-Smith Collection)

Olympic outward bound for New York sometime after her massive 1913 refit, passing the famous Hythe Pier, which still exists today complete with a miniature electric railroad to take passengers to the water. The end of the pier is one of the best vantage points to take pictures of the large cruise liners leaving port. (LuxuryLinerRow.com)

Olympic departing New York in 1914 with future United States President Herbert Hoover on board. Large crowds of people to see a liner off was a common site in the age of the Atlantic Ferry. Well-known maritime author Bill Miller has quipped that these days it is tough to find anyone to drive you to the airport!

Many changes have taken place to the liner since her introduction into service. Aside from the additional lifeboats, the most notable is the compass added over her bridge. This was a direct result of the findings after the British *Titanic* Inquiry. It was felt that it took too long for the crew to go aft to check the ship's main compass, which was on a platform over the raised roof of the first-class Lounge. As expected, this new compass over the bridge became the most used, and her midship compass platform was eventually removed sometime around 1926. (National Park Service, Harpers Ferry Center)

CHAPTER 3

THE GLORY THAT WAS *OLYMPIC*

The following pages: One of the most beautiful rooms afloat, the first-class *à la carte* Restaurant was an exclusive haunt for the the well-to-do among *Olympic*'s passengers. This room, decorated in the style of Louis XVI, was paneled in French walnut with the details of the carving beautifully gilded. Originally open from 8 a.m. to 11 p.m., meals were extra, and passengers who took their meals here exclusively were given a rebate on their passage fare of up to $25 depending on the price they paid for their cabin – the more expensive cabins received a higher rebate. In the 1920s, the Restaurant and the adjacent *Café Parisien* became the ship's night club. Dancing began at 11:15 p.m., and the rooms were open all night for dancing and light refreshments. Fortunately, much of the woodwork from this room is now on board the Celebrity *Millennium* as the *Olympic* Restaurant.

The question of china for this room occupied White Star for several months. After examining several china pattern samples, on January 17, 1911, White Star decided to use fine-quality bone china by Royal Crown Derby. When Stoniers (White Star's china broker) informed Royal Crown Derby of the decision, there was a caveat: '[White Star] … on figuring out the price, find that the order will amount to far more than they had anticipated, and unless we can meet them by a substantial reduction, they fear they will not be able to entertain the idea of adopting this china. They ask us to mention the fact that the supplying of this china to their steamers will be a world-wide advertisement for the Royal Crown Derby Co., as the cream of the passenger traffic will be carried on these steamers …'

Royal Crown Derby replied on January 23 saying that they had already 'fully considered and allowed for advertisement accruing. Regret impossible to concede any abatement in prices, which are rock-bottom.'

The china was reasonably priced and extremely high quality, and despite White Star's fuss about the cost, they went ahead with the purchase, even though they could not obtain a further discount. The cost for the initial order totaled £301 13s 6d and included the following pieces: 600 dinner plates, 150 soup plates, 150 breakfast plates, 100 salad plates, 150 breakfast cups and saucers, 100 tea cups and saucers, 35 creams, 25 slop basins. Stoniers also told Royal Crown Derby that: 'In addition to these quantities, we should have to keep a reserve stock for replacing breakages each voyage.'

Of special interest is that the pattern became exclusive to White Star when Royal Crown Derby removed it from general circulation at White Star's request. In the pattern books still held by Royal Crown Derby, there is a note from February, 1911, stating that the pattern is 'reserved' and that it was no longer to be shown on the general market.

White Star ordered this lovely china for the *à la carte* Restaurants of both *Olympic* and *Titanic*, and Royal Crown Derby was so proud of their association with the new liners that they printed 2,000 small brochures describing the Restaurant and the china they supplied to *Olympic*. The total cost to print these now highly collectible booklets was £8 3s 0d.

By the end of 1913, when the question was considered of what china pattern to use in *Britannic*'s Restaurant, price reared its ugly head again, and White Star decided to use a different non-Royal Crown Derby pattern. Stoniers' final word on this is interesting: 'We must say we were very much astonished at our client's choice, as the pattern they have selected could not, by any stretch of the imagination, be considered to have any relation to the Louis XVI style of decorations and furnishings which will be adopted in the restaurant on the new steamer.' It was a rather frank assessment of the decision for *Britannic*.

White Star continued to use the Royal Crown Derby china in the Restaurant of *Olympic* until the start of World War I. After the war, the pattern was abandoned, White Star deciding to use a less expensive pattern from another supplier. (Alex Cheek Collection)

The china pattern for the *à la carte* Restaurant as it appears in the pattern book of Royal Crown Derby and a photo showing some samples of the china as produced. An egg cup and a crescent salad plate identical to the ones shown here were recovered from the debris field at *Titanic*'s wreck site. (Royal Crown Derby Archives, LuxuryLinerRow.com)

One of the most popular innovations on the *Olympic*-class liners was a reception room just forward of the Dining Room where passengers could gather to have afternoon tea, listen to concerts, or spend a leisurely afternoon conversing with their shipmates. This room proved to be so popular on *Olympic* that White Star decided to enlarge it. Oddly, despite the popularity of this room, the concept was not frequently copied by competing lines.

The biggest weakness of Victorian and Edwardian ocean liners, at least to many modern travelers, was the lack of activities on board. *Olympic* was one of the first transatlantic ships to address the issue of boredom by offering amenities like cafés, a restaurant, a reception room, a gymnasium, a Turkish bath, barber shops, a pool, squash court, and by the 1920s, shops, hairdressers, movies, and dance floors. While other ships may have pioneered one or two of these diversions for passengers at sea, *Olympic* was the first to incorporate so many choices. On *Lusitania*, for example, a passenger could never have a massage, play squash, or go to the gym. *Olympic* had so many passenger amenities that she set the standard for British liners for decades to come, and with few refinements, a passenger on *Olympic* would have felt right at home on the *Queen Mary* in 1936.

It is remarkable how well preserved this room is in the wreck of *Titanic*. This area of the ship flooded so slowly that the decorative features are still in situ. The leaded-glass arched windows are nearly all intact and even such delicate items as the planter on the right-hand side of the photo is still in place.

The inset photo shows a sampling of the wicker furniture still at the manufacturer. (Alex Cheek Collection)

This page: One of the few criticisms leveled at *Olympic* was her lack of a double-height Dining Room. It doesn't appear that White Star ever intended for her to have a two-deck Dining Room like her competition. This would have taken away the prime midships cabin space just above on C deck, where some of the nicest and priciest accommodations on the ship were eventually located. The earliest general arrangement plans that still exist for *Olympic* show her Dining Room with a large dome overhead, similar to earlier White Star ships like *Teutonic*, *Oceanic*, and the Big Four of *Celtic*, *Cedric*, *Adriatic* and *Baltic*. As the design progressed, however, White Star decided on a single-level room with no dome, which was more suited to the Jacobean style chosen to decorate the space. Despite the room's vertical limitations, the designers did not disappoint. It was the largest room afloat, sporting ten-foot ceilings which still lent an air of spaciousness.

One of the two views shown here is *c.* 1911, and the second view dates to the late 1920s. The post-war view looks aft while the pre-war view shows the forward end of the room, which lead into the Reception Room. In the 1920s image, the dance floor clearly shows one of the changes made in the post-Edwardian era. Dancing in the 1920s had become a favorite pastime of many; so on *Olympic*, dance floors were added in several of the first- and second-class lounges as well as in the first-class Dining Room. (J&C McCutcheon Collection, Brian Hawley Collection)

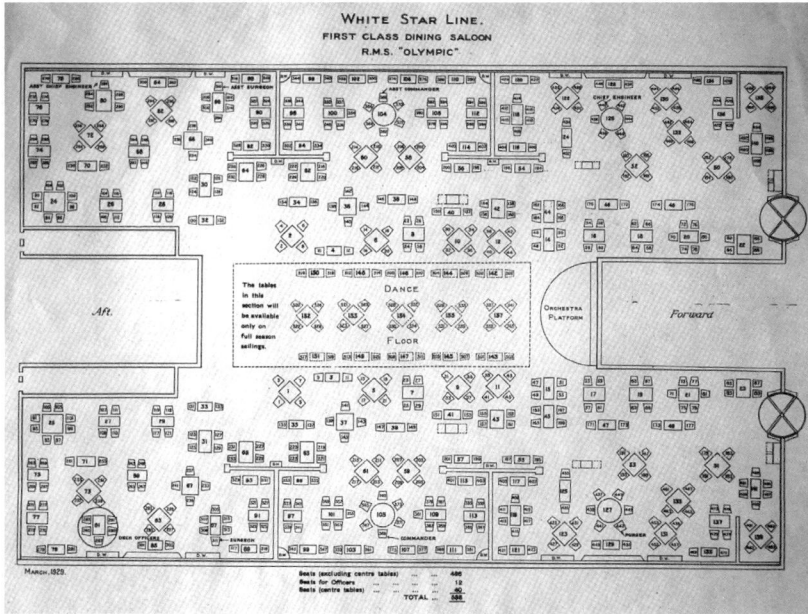

One of the only known plans for Olympic's dining room. Dated March, 1929, the plan shows the locations of the senior officers' tables as well as the number of people that could be accomodated in the room. During high-capacity summer sailings, dining tables could be set up on the recently installed dance floor. (John White, White Star Memories Collection)

C-59 was a period French revival, oak-paneled suite, designed and decorated by Harland & Wolff, not an outside decorative firm. Although not as elaborate as some of the cabins on the same deck, it was near some of the finest suites on board. This accommodation surpassed all that had come before on the Atlantic in size and comfort. White Star was among the first (if not the first) to provide double beds in some of their larger cabins instead of twin beds. Even as late as the 1960s, when the *Queen Elizabeth 2* was built, nearly all cabins at sea had twin beds. Gertrude Vanderbilt sailed in this very cabin in the early 1920s. In 1922 for a high-season crossing, this room, including the bath, cost $1,490 for two. (Harland & Wolff, Alex Cheek Collection)

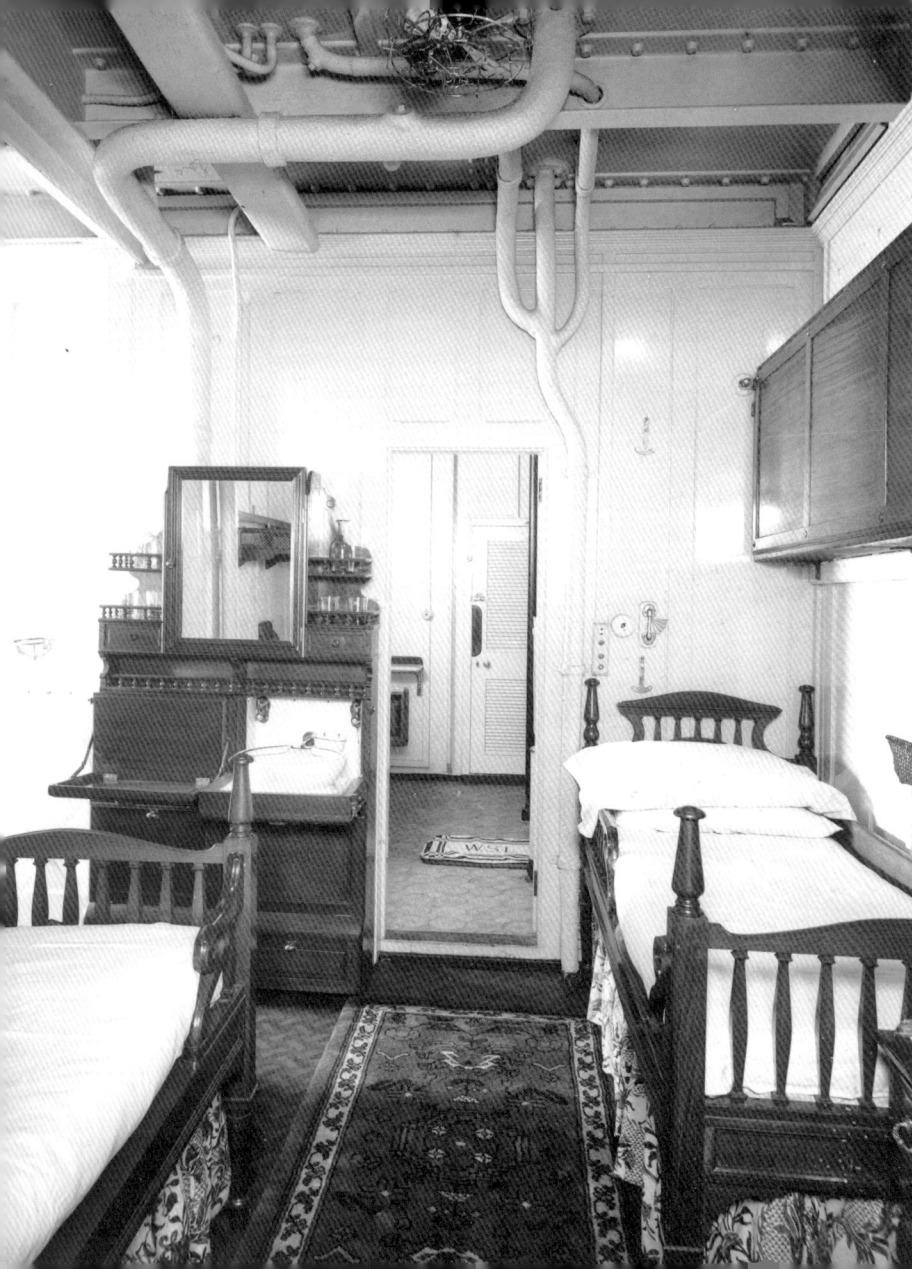

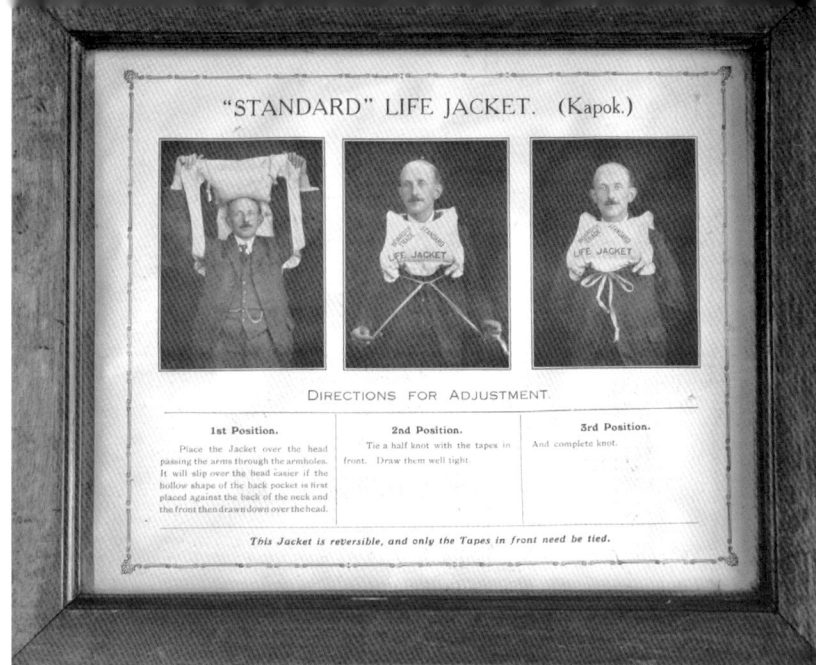

"STANDARD" LIFE JACKET. (Kapok.)

DIRECTIONS FOR ADJUSTMENT.

1st Position.	2nd Position.	3rd Position.
Place the Jacket over the head passing the arms through the armholes. It will slip over the head easier if the hollow shape of the back pocket is first placed against the back of the neck and the front then drawn down over the head.	Tie a half knot with the tapes in front. Draw them well tight.	And complete knot.

This Jacket is reversible, and only the Tapes in front need be tied.

Left: A typical first-class cabin on D Deck, D-19. This type of cabin was nicknamed a 'Bibby' cabin and was named after the line that invented them. Bibby cabins were inside staterooms that had been turned into outside staterooms by taking a bit of space from the neighboring outside cabin and creating a corridor that lead to the porthole from the inside cabin. This arrangement allowed more outside cabins that could be booked for higher fares. This photo, taken in 1920, also shows the addition of a bathroom that was made by cannibalizing an inside stateroom. (Alex Cheek Collection)

Above: An original 1920s lifejacket instruction sign from a stateroom on *Olympic*. (Brian Hawley Collection)

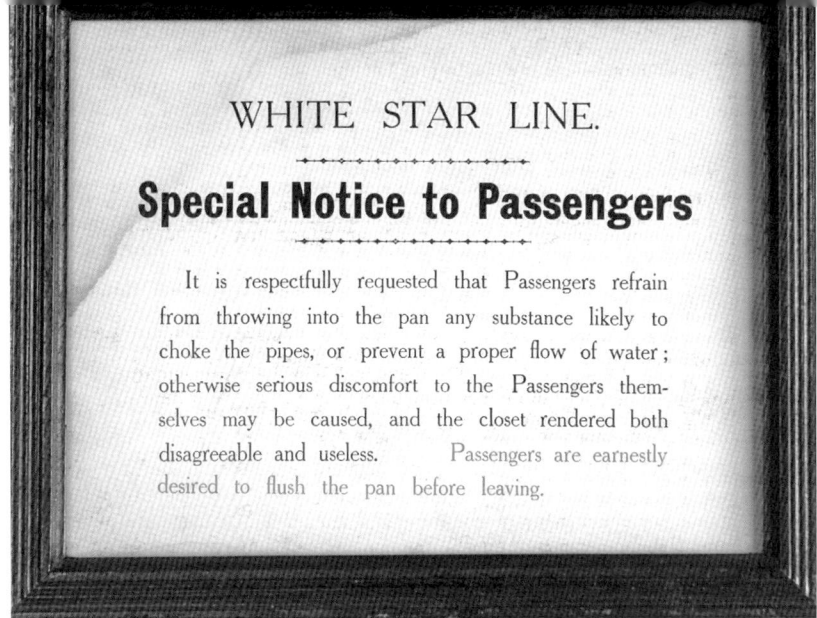

WHITE STAR LINE.

Special Notice to Passengers

It is respectfully requested that Passengers refrain from throwing into the pan any substance likely to choke the pipes, or prevent a proper flow of water; otherwise serious discomfort to the Passengers themselves may be caused, and the closet rendered both disagreeable and useless.   Passengers are earnestly desired to flush the pan before leaving.

Left: As ship building progressed, the number of private baths on board liners increased as the ships became larger and as passengers discovered the benefit of not having to go down the hall to use the facilities. For example, the *Oceanic* of 1899 had only two cabins with private baths in her first-class accommodation. By the time the *Queen Mary* entered service in 1936, every first-class stateroom had private facilities. When *Olympic* was built, many of her first-class cabins did not have private baths, but during each overhaul starting with the 1913 refit, more bathrooms were added to her first-class accommodations to meet the increased demand for private facilities. This bathroom on *Olympic* was attached to C-58. (Harland & Wolff, Braxton Williams Collection)

Above: An unusual notice that hung over one of the toilets on board *Olympic*. (LuxuryLinerRow.com)

Above, left and right: Although very well designed and laid out, *Olympic* still was not immune from changes and/or improvements, and many of these were brought about by the changes in immigration laws in the early 1920s. This view of the second-class Dining Room shows one of the most important changes. Visible in the distance on the center right-hand side of the room is the wall which created the new 'tourist-third' Dining Room. Tourist third was made up of the low-end second-class accommodation combined with the best of the former third class and offered at lower rates than second class. This caused a shuffle of public rooms to provide for the new class. All of this effort was an attempt to increase passenger traffic following the dismal levels seen after 1923. (Eric Sauder Collection)

Above left: Just as in first class, the second-class accommodation on board *Olympic* was distinguished by expansive public rooms. Being half again as large as her nearest competitor, she was able to offer her passengers unrivaled amounts of space in all classes. Here in her second-class Smoking Room on B Deck aft, gentlemen retired after dinner for cigars and games of cards. Several fittings from this room are known to survive, including the bar pass through from the aft port corner, some paneling, and several of the window surrounds. (Alex Cheek Collection)

Above right: This two-berth, second-class cabin includes a sofa under the porthole that was convertible to two berths for high-season sailings. Second-class did not enjoy the luxury of standalone beds, only bunks, and there was no running water in the staterooms. In many instances in second class, the cabin was shared with strangers. Each berth in the stateroom was given a number which corresponded to a numbered disc just above each hook to the left of the wash basin so you would not accidentally use someone else's towel.

The fold-down wash basin, or compactum, was a very common sight on all lines, even in first class. Made of mahogany, they served a number of purposes. On either side of the mirror and held in place by the railings were drinking glasses and water decanters. The mirror hid the galvanized tank of fresh water from which the wash basin was filled. At the top of the compactum on the right-hand side of the mirror, the funnel used to fill the tank can be seen. Gravity fed water from the tank into the basin, the flow of which was controlled by the spigot seen peeking between each set of soap dishes. Because the basins had no drains in their bottoms like modern-day sinks, to empty the water, the basin was folded up into the cabinet. This operation had to be done slowly to allow the water to empty over the back rim of the bowl and drain out the back into galvanized tanks below, which were emptied by the cabin steward. Raising the basin up too quickly practically guaranteed wet feet. Since the compactum was not plumbed, it only provided cold water. If hot water were required, the passenger contacted his steward, who brought a brass pitcher of hot water. The pitcher can be seen here hanging on the right. (Alex Cheek Collection)

Utilitarian in design, this was the main third-class staircase on C Deck. The door to the right is the entrance to the Smoking Room, and that on the left is the entrance to the General Room. Third-class accommodation was simply no-frills practicality. Interestingly, despite the devastating destruction of this area on the stern of *Titanic*'s wreck, a few tiles of this identical linoleum pattern can still be seen in place. (Harland & Wolff, Alex Cheek Collection)

Spartan and unadorned, there is no hint of the luxurious nature of the suites just a few decks above. The third-class cabins were definitely basic, but even here in her lowest class, *Olympic* excelled. Her third-class cabins were far superior to her competition because, on most liners, third-class passengers were generally berthed in spaces holding up to ten people, and usually more, in dormitory-style rooms. The better cabins in *Olympic*'s third class positioned the ship well when much of third class was converted to tourist third in the 1920s. (LuxuryLinerRow.com)

CHAPTER 4

A LINER DISGUISED

Olympic arrived in New York on August 5, 1914, just after war broke out. Her scheduled crossing back to Southampton (on which only 125 passengers had booked) was canceled, and on August 9, she sailed with only crew, arriving in Liverpool on August 15. She made two further voyages to New York, but from Liverpool instead of Southampton. On October 27, she sighted the battleship HMS *Audacious*, which had struck a German mine and was sinking. *Olympic*'s crew bravely rescued hundreds of sailors from the doomed battleship. After this voyage, she was laid up in Belfast very near her sister *Britannic*, which was then fitting out. After nearly a year in lay up, *Olympic* began her first trooping voyage on September 23, 1915, with the official number T2810.

This photo shows the transport in Mudros, Greece, near the end of 1915. She was outfitted to carry nearly 6,000 troops per voyage to the ill-fated Gallipoli campaign. In an odd twist, as *Olympic* brought out a fresh load of troops for battle, her sister *Britannic* took the wounded home. (Rene Bergeron Collection)

Olympic in Halifax. White Star had a long association with the Admiralty going back to *Teutonic* and *Majestic* of 1889. In return for operating subsidies, White Star incorporated certain features into the design of those ships which facilitated converting them into armed merchant cruisers should the need arise, and making the liners available for government use. Shortly after International Mercantile Marine (IMM) came into being, they signed an agreement with the British government that ensured British ships would be made available during time of war, even though the line was being taken over by American interests. (Rene Bergeron Collection)

Above: The British government had problems utilizing the big liners early in the war. It was originally intended that they be used as armed auxiliary cruisers and go on war patrols, but the government soon discovered that operating such large vessels as warships was impractical. The big ships' vast requirements of coal, crew, and fresh water, not to mention large deep-water docks, dramatically reduced their appeal to the Royal Navy. It was eventually decided that the liners were best utilized as troop transports and hospital ships. (George Behe Collection)

Top right and bottom: Two photos taken on August 3, 1918, while *Olympic* was docked at Pier 59 in Manhattan. She was on trooping service and had been warped out from the pier to allow for coaling. The idea for 'dazzle' paint is credited to famed English artist Norman Wilkinson. The thought was that a series of geometric shapes painted on a ship's hull in black, blue, white, and grey would confuse enemy submarines, making it difficult to determine the ship's size, speed, and heading. In theory, the idea might have worked. In reality, though, maintaining the paint scheme was time consuming and expensive. It seems that grey was the best camouflage for ships on the North Atlantic, and dazzle painting was not used to a large extent during World War II. (National Archives and Records Administration)

The third in the series of images taken on that same day in August, 1918. This set of photos was used by the U.S. Navy to determine if dazzle-paint schemes were effective. The Navy makes a special note of how dirty the ship was and how difficult it was to maintain the dazzle paint. The ship is in her first dazzle scheme. (National Archives and Records Administration)

Olympic was painted in two different dazzle designs during the war. The following images are U.S. Navy drawings produced to help identify foreign shipping and as an aid in studying the effectiveness of dazzle paint.

The first port-side dazzle scheme for *Olympic*. (National Archives and Records Administration)

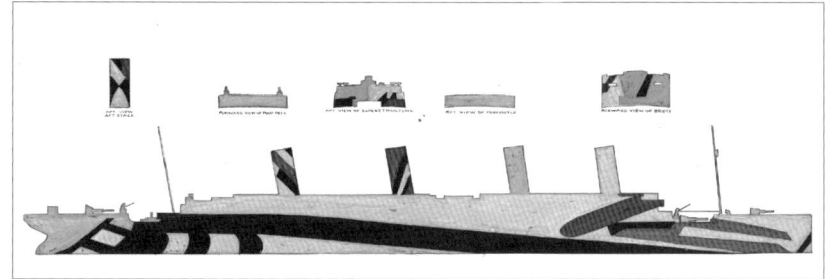

The first starboard-side dazzle scheme for *Olympic*. (National Archives and Records Administration)

This sketch of *Olympic* was made by Percy Hale Lund, Seaman 2nd Class, while on board the USS *Amphitrite* at 6:00 p.m., February 10, 1918. The drawing was done in overcast weather from about one-half mile away and shows the ship in dazzle Type 19, Design A, the first of the two patterns she wore. (National Archives and Records Administration)

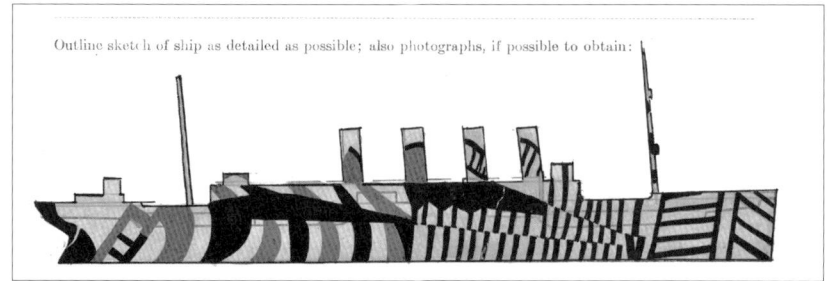

This sketch shows the second of her guises and was also made from the USS *Amphitrite*. Percy Lund produced this drawing at 1:05 p.m., September 10, 1918, in clear weather from one mile away. The colors used on *Olympic*'s hull, as indicated in the Navy notes, are black, No. 3 blue, and No. 1 blue gray. This pattern was Type 19, Design AX and is far more distinctive than the previous style. (National Archives and Records Administration)

Olympic is said to have carried nearly 8,000 troops on one of her runs to Gallipoli in the Dardanelles, giving her the distinction of carrying the most people on any one ship up to that time. The record today for embarking the largest number of souls on a liner belongs to the Cunard liner *Queen Mary*. On one voyage during World War II, she carried just over 16,000 people. Here, *Olympic* is painted in dazzle scheme No. 2, which was the last pattern used. (Rene Bergeron Collection)

Taken on October 18, 1918, by Seaman 2nd Class S.F. Scott, the next few photos show *Olympic* docked in New York in her second dazzle guise. Note that many of her lower, forward portholes on F and G decks have been plated over. Open ports, especially low in the ship, were a major problem during the war and greatly contributed to the rapid sinking of the Cunarder *Lusitania* and *Olympic*'s own sister ship *Britannic*. The rest of the ports were painted over so the ship was completely blacked out at night.

In January, 1918, *Olympic* left New York for her first trooping voyage from that port. On board was Jack Franklin, son of IMM President P.A.S. Franklin. Jack went on to become head of the United States Lines, the successor to IMM. (National Archives and Records Administration)

In an unusual view from the roof of Pier 59, one of the six-inch guns on her forecastle is clearly visible. Note the care taken with the geometric shapes in this dazzle scheme. The superstructure, funnels, guns, and even the crow's nest gets the dazzle treatment. Lined up on the forward end of A Deck are what appear to be civilians who have come to visit the ship! (National Archives and Records Administration)

The torpedo-shaped device in front of the crew in the well deck is a paravane. It was suspended over the side of the ship, attached by chains to the bow, and was used to cut the mooring chains on mines. (National Archives and Records Administration)

These two photos were taken on November 10, 1918, the day before the end of World War I, as *Olympic* is warped into the pier. If there had been crowds to greet her and no dazzle paint, this could almost be the maiden voyage arrival. Her funnels tower over the home booms, the scaffolding for working cargo, which rise above the roof of the pier. (National Archives and Records Administration)

Above: Olympic slowly makes her way up Halifax Harbour at the end of a repatriation voyage crammed with Canadian troops. Of all the big ships in World War I, *Olympic* had a special association with Halifax and the Canadian Expeditionary Force, carrying over 80,000 Canadians to fight in the Great War. (Rene Bergeron Collection)

Left: The 25th Battalion arriving at Halifax on May 16, 1919. Making the most of the moment, thousands of jubilant Canadian troops are everywhere, even on the roofs of her wing bridges. In August, 1919, *Olympic* returned to her builders for her post-war refit. Her five years of war service saw her travel 180,000 miles, carry 200,000 troops, attempt to save a sinking battleship, and sink the German submarine *U-103*. She earned and deserved her nickname, the 'Old Reliable'. (Rene Bergeron Collection)

Anchored in Halifax, having just discharged another contingent of homeward-bound Canadian troops, *Olympic* looks a bit ragged even though she has been repainted in company colors. The action of the sea has worn the paint off the bow revealing a hint of her last dazzle scheme, and her wartime signal lamps on either side of A Deck just under the bridge wing are still in place. (Rene Bergeron Collection)

CHAPTER 5

'NOBLEST STEAMSHIP OF THEM ALL ...'

Left: Olympic was the ship to beat in the early 1920s. Here she is seen freshly painted and sporting loads of nested lifeboats. 1919–23 were excellent years for all the big liners, and immigration, although not as high as pre-war levels, still boomed. The advantage for both White Star and Cunard was the total absence of German competition.

In many ways, *Olympic* led the way with innovation. Notably, she was the first of the big liners to be converted to oil fuel, and *The New York Times* said that she ushered in the 'oil age'. Although oil cost more than coal and the costs to convert a ship to burn oil were high, the savings in time loading fuel, cleaning up the coal dust, and the vast reduction in boiler-room crew more than made up for the expenditure. (The Mariners' Museum)

Right: The forward end of Boat Deck was reserved for officers and was a place passengers usually weren't allowed. The gentleman on the right, obviously a crew member and perhaps a steward, was probably assigned to give these VIPs a tour of the vessel. Note the vast changes in lifeboat equipment since 1911.

Just to the right of the crew member is the entrance door to the officers' quarters, and the four windows between the cameraman and the door (going left to right) are the captain's bathroom, bedroom, and day room (last two windows on right). Compare this image to the one on page 14, showing the same area of the liner. (John White, White Star Memories Collection)

Above: The rails lined with passengers, and another crossing begins. A superb atmospheric shot of *Olympic* leaving her pier in New York in the middle of the 1920s. (Peter Davies-Garner Collection)

Right: Being nursed out of Pier 59 in New York *c.* 1921. This perspective is what one might have seen while sitting on the iceberg on that fateful April night in 1912.

One of the most enjoyable aspects of sailing on one's favorite ship time after time is seeing the same crew members and being recognized as a past passenger. *Olympic*'s crew was all British and in many cases had sailed on her for years at a time. They built a reputation for service so strong that the sense of coming home became a powerful marketing tool that helped greatly with *Olympic*'s popularity. (The Mariners' Museum)

Left: (J&C McCutcheon Collection)

A distinguishing feature of the White Star fleet was a yellow-gold painted sheer line located between the white upper works and the black of the hull. In 1922, when the German-built *Majestic* and *Homeric* entered White Star service, the company lowered the sheer line on all of their ships. Here, *Olympic* is seen in Southampton's Ocean Dock in the late 1920s with the lowered sheer line. (The Mariners' Museum)

Saturday, March 22, 1924. As *Olympic* backed out of her New York pier, the Furness Bermuda Liner *Fort St George*, which might have been racing a rival Bermuda bound liner, the *Arcadian*, collided with *Olympic*, striking her stern. At first it was thought *Olympic* suffered only some scuffed paint; so she continued her crossing. Soon, however, it became clear that her stern post had been fractured in the collision. This was very bad news indeed for White Star. The stern post, which weighed 70 tons, was a major part of her structure that supported the rudder and center propeller. Replacing one had never been carried out on such a large ship before.

Substantial amounts of shell plating around the stern post had to be stripped off to accomplish the repair. The letters, seen here chalked on her side, each represent a strake, or the 'strips' of plating that make up her hull. Replacing the stern post was very costly and unfortunately did not work out as well as planned. The steel in the new post reacted poorly with the older surrounding steel, and the new steel became severely pitted, necessitating its repair on a few occasions. Harland & Wolff patched the problem, but the trouble with the condition of the ship's hull must have played a roll in the decision to scrap the ship ten years later. (David Hutchings Collection)

Ever since their bankruptcy in 1915, the International Mercantile Marine (IMM) had been unsuccessfully attempting to sell White Star. IMM had never been the strong force envisioned during the company's formation because, among other reasons, they counted heavily on American subsidies that never materialized. The company was never very profitable because of massive debts and heavy dividend payouts, forcing IMM into bankruptcy just thirteen years after acquiring White Star. In 1919, an attempt to sell White Star was squelched by President Wilson on national security grounds.

In 1926, IMM accepted an offer for White Star's assets from the well-run Furness Withy Line. Furness Withy shrewdly put a clause in the contract that stated the purchase of White Star would become void if England suffered a general strike before the merger was complete. Regrettably, a strike came to pass in May, 1926, the contract was voided, and IMM was forced to seek a new buyer. By November of that same year, P.A.S. Franklin, IMM's president, concluded the sale of White Star to the Royal Mail group. This fateful transaction sealed the fate of White Star.

Royal Mail, the new owners of *Olympic*, were in a difficult position by the late 1920s. Outwardly, the company appeared solid as a rock; the core, however, was rotten. Royal Mail had been building debts and suffering losses for years and hiding them in a complicated accounting and shareholding scheme. The subterfuge came out when Royal Mail went bankrupt. Lord Kylsant, the company's president, was convicted of fraud and sent to jail. Peter Boyd-Smith Collection)

Opposite: Southampton's Ocean Dock in 1928. (Peter Boyd-Smith Collection)

During the early 1930s, Cunard made several attempts to purchase the Atlantic assets of White Star but was never able to complete the deal. Negotiations went back and forth over time with various proposals being floated by each line, but they always ended with no agreement being reached. Aside from cost, one of the main factors that stopped Cunard's takeover was that Cunard was trying to cherry pick White Star's assets to eliminate competition. Because of the immigration quotas, inflated post-war shipbuilding costs, and in White Star's case, outright mismanagement, neither Cunard nor White Star was strong enough to complete a merger on their own. The British government finally stepped in and 'helped' bring about a merger in 1934. At the end of the government-led negotiations, Cunard wound up the dominant partner, owning 62 per cent of the shares in the new company; and White Star, a mere 38 per cent. This was based on the value of the two fleets in the government's opinion after much back and forth between the government and Cunard. The merger of the two former rivals was completed on January 1, 1934, but no announcement was made until May, 1934.

Eventually, and somewhat surprisingly, the Cunard White Star merger was a textbook success. Corporate history is littered with two weak companies being merged into one and still failing spectacularly. The vast cost savings and efficiencies that came about from selling off old ships and replacing them with far fewer modern vessels resulted in the most successful pair of liners ever built – the *Queen Mary* and *Queen Elizabeth*. The two-ship service that the new company was able to institute after World War II made so much money that Cunard White Star was able to pay off its massive debts of at least £8 million, catch up its share holders on dividends that had not been paid from 1930 until 1944, and pay back White Star's creditors by 1949 – something no one thought possible in the early 1930s.

The bleaker side of the merger was that White Star officers very rarely received promotions within the new Cunard White Star. It was a very sad state of affairs for former White Star employees because the same thing had happened in 1927 when Royal Mail officers received promotion preference over long-serving White Star officers. In both mergers White Star staff saw a lifetime of good and faithful service jerked out from under them with no hope of further advancement, and there was nothing they could do to stop it. (John White, White Star Memories Collection)

Above: A superb aerial view of Southampton's Ocean Dock taken about 1931. Docked with *Olympic* are *Homeric* and *Aquitania*. The two-funneled ship to *Olympic*'s starboard side across the quay is White Star's *Doric*, dressed overall and preparing to depart on a cruise.

Olympic was by far the most successful of White Star's post-war trio and was the biggest money maker for White Star, even more so than the new *Majestic*. Because *Olympic* made so much money on the North Atlantic, the company couldn't, and almost never did, pull her off that route for extended periods of cruising in the 1920s. They left that to the smaller and slower ships, particularly *Homeric*, which was the least successful of the post-war White Star trio. In many ways, White Star probably would have been better off not taking *Homeric* after the war and building their own new liner in 1919. (Peter Boyd-Smith Collection)

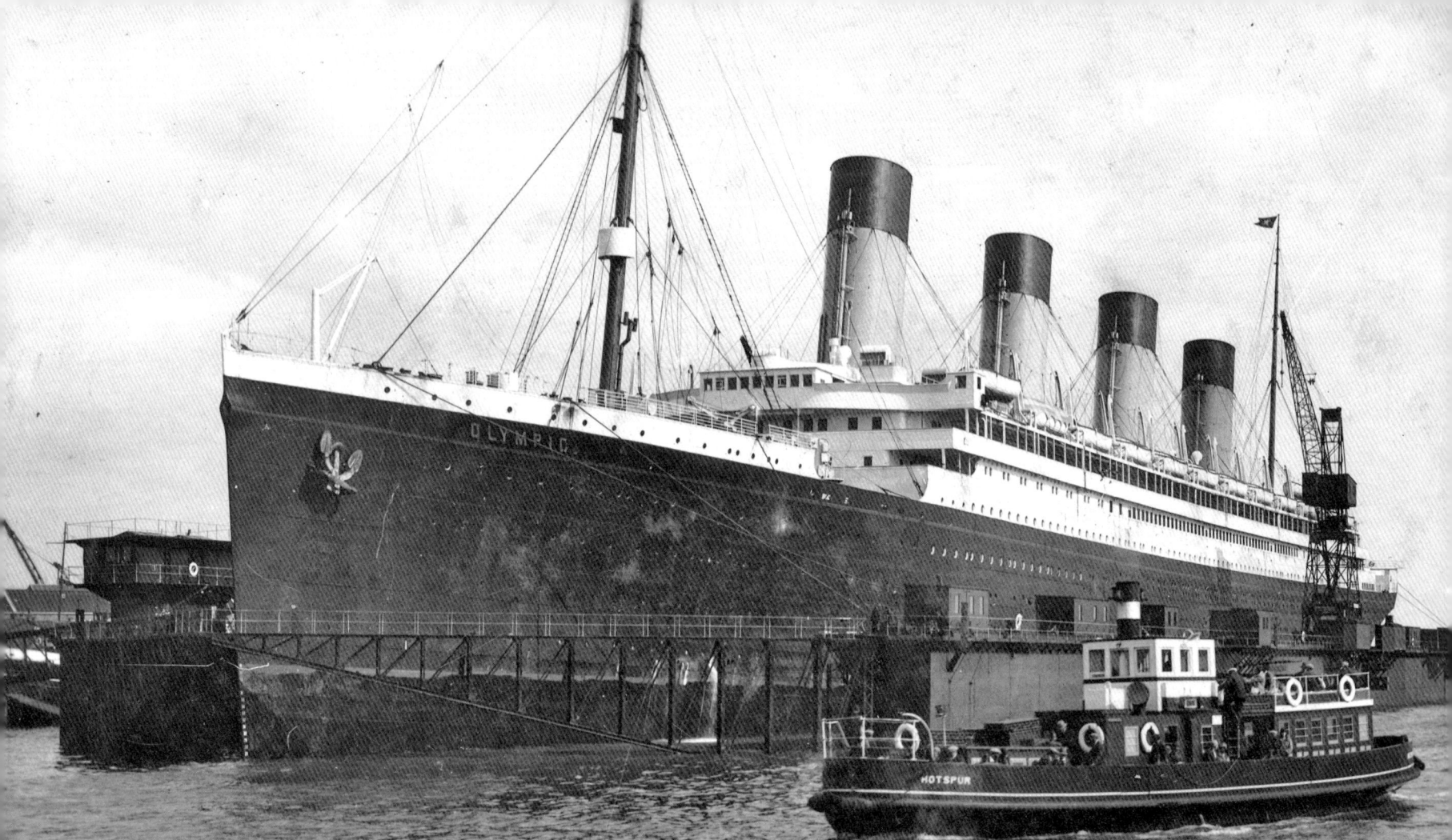

OLYMPIC

HOTSPUR

SISTER SHIPS.

Opposite: Originally, the letters of *Olympic*'s name were not bolted on to the hull. Rather, the outline of each letter was cut into the shell plating and then filled in with paint. Late in her career, however, perhaps in an attempt to make her appear more modern, the letters of her name were changed to much larger italicized brass ones affixed to the hull. During her 1927/1928 refit, a number of new cabins were added to B Deck forward when the first-class accommodation was extended to the sides of the liner. Originally, this had been enclosed promenade space. Compare this view to earlier photos to see how the rectangular windows on B Deck forward have been changed to pairs of portholes. (LuxuryLinerRow.com)

Above: By this time all the main line ships in the fleets of Cunard and White Star were aging, and the new vessels coming into service were quickly eclipsing the old Edwardian liners. The competition was heating up dramatically as traffic fell even further with the onset of the Depression. *Olympic*'s period interiors, which were very popular in 1911, could hardly hold up to the ultra-modern interiors of the *Ile de France* of the French Line. The *Ile De France* of 1927 was huge step forward decoratively and was vastly different from the pre-war ships. Her Art Deco interiors were so modern that they made *Olympic*'s interiors seem terribly outmoded. White Star made several attempts to update *Olympic*'s interiors, but the reality was that she was getting left behind by the competition. (Peter Boyd-Smith Collection)

CHAPTER 6

THE END OF THE LINE

Above: Laid up in late 1935 at Pier 108 in Southampton's new Western Docks. The Depression had exacerbated an already large overabundance of shipping. Traffic was down nearly 50 per cent from 1929, and for the newly formed Cunard White Star, there was just no need for six express liners to maintain a weekly service to New York. The traffic simply wasn't there to support them.

Despite her 24 years and deferred maintenance over the prior few months, she still looked magnificent as she towered above the docks. Even at this point, *Olympic* was still one of the largest ships in the world. Note the canvas caps on her forward two funnels. The third funnel was not covered during layup because those boilers were required to provide power for the ship. (The Mariners' Museum)

Opposite right: *Olympic*'s days were numbered almost as soon as Cunard and White Star merged in May, 1934, and she was axed in the first round of reorganization. Some researchers have argued that she should have been left in service and that Cunarders which had more mechanical issues should have been retired. This is a very reasonable stance, but mergers tend to have one company that is dominant, and in this case, it was very much the Cunard side of Cunard White Star. (Eric Sauder Collection)

Above: Cunard White Star announced that *Olympic* would be opened on August 20, 1935, for inspection by prospective purchasers. Less than three weeks later, she was purchased by industrialist and philanthropist Sir John Jarvis to help alleviate unemployment in Jarrow. Her fate was now sealed. *Olympic* sailed from Southampton for the final time at 4 p.m. on October 11, 1935. She arrived on the Tyne late Saturday evening, the 12th, but because of tidal conditions, had to wait until Sunday to make her final passage to the breaking yard. Jarvis had paid £97,500 for the ship. This view shows her arriving on the Tyne. (J&C McCutcheon Collection)

Olympic made quite a splash on Tyneside when she arrived, drawing huge crowds because of her fame and size. Because of the depression in shipbuilding and the collapse of Palmers Yard in Jarrow in 1933, the area was suffering nearly 80 per cent unemployment. Despite Jarvis's good intentions in trying to help alleviate local unemployment, not surprisingly, opposition politicians complained that the jobs Jarvis created by the scrapping of *Olympic* were just a token move on his part to curry favor, considering only a few hundred at best would find employment. (Titanic International Society, Joe Carvalho Collection)

This view of *Olympic* is reminiscent of the well-known view of her sister *Titanic* leaving Harland & Wolff on her trials twenty-three years before. Despite making her final trip to her ultimate demise, *Olympic* is still impressive. (Titanic International Society, Joe Carvalho Collection)

With just feet to go before she was tied up and would never again move under her own power, *Olympic* is slowly eased into the ship-breaking berth.

From 10 to 5 on October 31, the liner was opened for private viewing by prospective bidders upon presentation of an auction catalogue for which they had paid five shillings. The ship then went on public view on Friday, Saturday, and Monday, November 1, 2, and 4 from 10 to 5 to those who had paid two shillings and six pence for their catalogue. The auction took place over ten days at Palmers Yard in Jarrow from Tuesday, November 5, to Monday, November 18, starting at 11 o'clock sharp each day.

Because it was the middle of the Depression, many purchasers were looking for cheap fittings to outfit their offices and hotels and even remodel their homes. We are fortunate that a large number of fittings from *Olympic* survive and have been making appearances over the last few decades. The first major auction of items from *Olympic* since 1935 was held in Newcastle in December, 1991, when a number of important fittings were found in a barn, where they had been stored for fifty-six years. The seller's father had purchased leftovers at the 1935 disbursal sale with the intention of remodeling a room in his home. This never came to pass, and the fittings remained in storage until they once again came to the auction block. The two most important items sold that day were the clock panel from the aft grand staircase (still in its green paint from the 1933 refit) and the forward entrance doors to the first-class Lounge. (Titanic International Society, Joe Carvalho Collection)

Opposite left: This amazing view of the forward first-class staircase was taken just as the auction house began to strip *Olympic* of her fittings. The famous cherub is already gone. This exquisite staircase, which is widely considered the finest ever installed on any liner, was controversially painted green, as this article from *The Ocean Ferry* of 1933 explains:

After an absence of several months, the famous White Star liner Olympic arrived at New York on March 8 from Cherbourg and Southampton, in a gorgeous new dress of pale green and gold, looking like a debutante and apparently feeling as sprightly.

Her arrival was eagerly awaited by the press and many of her old friends among the general public, to whom the Olympic is not merely a ship, but an institution.

After the first feeling of surprise at the daring change which has been made in her scheme of decoration, it was agreed on all sides that the new ideas incorporated into the interior design had greatly enhanced her beauty. The Olympic's staff was much enthused; they admitted that they liked the change. And sailormen are usually frank.

Chief among the many new features are the entire overhauling of the first class entrance halls and staircases and the modernization of staterooms. The job of redecorating the ship was handled by Ashby Tabb, of Heaton Tabb & Co., Ltd., of London, a recent visitor to New York on the maiden voyage of the new White Star motorship Georgic for whose decoration he was responsible.

Great thought and care were given to the Olympic's new dress, so as to preserve the spirit and tradition which has grown up around her. The first class staircases are superb in any guise, broad and dignified, and far beyond in magnificence any ship of recent years. They are designed in the quiet grandeur of the English tradition of the Georgian period, and readily lend themselves to a fine artistic scheme.

Preliminary models were made and decorated and taken on board for criticism and for study of the effects of the lighting. Many ideas were considered before it was decided to build up on a background of soft Georgian green, a harmony of color in quiet tones relieved with the rich bronze balustrade, some touches of gold on the more prominent carved cornices, leading up to a number of decorative panels of classical landscapes, which were specially painted and form points of interest in the design.

Great care was given to these panels, and many sketches were prepared so that the scale and character of the whole would be preserved. The panels were painted on board the ship because the artist felt that the atmosphere of the new surroundings would best be preserved if they were executed in the environment in which they were to appear.

There are now 127 staterooms with private baths, large numbers of outside rooms on B and C decks at minimum rates, and the tourist accommodation now includes many rooms with private bath.

Furniture and curtains have been renewed, and many new effects have been produced with rich pelmets and hangings. Among other improvements many of the first class staterooms have undergone a change and a lighter touch has been introduced in accordance with modern ideas.

With the Majestic, *world's largest ship, the Olympic will maintain the White Star Line's express service from New York to Cherbourg and Southampton. The* Homeric, *third unit of this service, is scheduled for a full program of cruises from England.* (Titanic International Society, Joe Carvalho Collection)

Inset: A photo of the staircase in happier times. (Alex Cheek Collection)

Opposite: The first-class Lounge as it appeared as the auction was proceeding, having been stripped of its furniture. This view looks forward, and the wooden dance floor in front of the fireplace was added as dancing became popular in the 1920s. The carpet has been removed from the rest of the room, showing the Litosilo subfloor, which was a composite material used to deaden sound and smooth out the deck for carpet. Much of this exquisite room, including paneling, fireplace, mirror, doors, and light fixtures, found a new home at the White Swan Hotel in Alnwick, England. Long a site of pilgrimage for *Olympic* and *Titanic* enthusiasts, it is quite amazing to see in person. The smaller archival is taken from almost at the exact same location twenty-four years previously, when the ship was new.

Here are the entries for this room from the 1935 auction catalogue:

3503 – The carved oak panelling throughout, with scroll floral and shell ornamentation, including a pair of doors with bevelled plate, upper panels having ornamental ormolu fittings, floor springs and stops, the exterior carved and painted in green and gilt, a carved and paneled post box with wire liner and two doors, the windows complete with leaded glass panels, fittings, etc., the outer windows with glazed panels and green canvas coverings, the eight partitions, four having plate-glass panels forming four alcoves, the carved oak door to dispense bar, with bevelled plate-glass panels, ormolu fittings, door spring and stop, the ditto to Port Corridor, two centre partitions, having shaped plate-glass panels, the grey carved marble mantelpiece and grey marble hearth, with iron fleur de lys fire back and shaped mirror over, the finely carved mahogany shaped bookcase with scroll and shell pediment, fitted shelves and enclosed by five glazed panelled doors with dwarf cupboards under enclosed by twelve panelled doors with ormolu fittings, 18 ft. overall, the painted and gilt decorated ceiling with scroll and musical instrument ornamentations with oval cupola, and the oak ceiling to the four supporting columns, 11 ft. 4 high, also the pierced brass pipe coverings at floor level, the ormolu bell presses, and the fitted cabin hooks, Overall measurements of Lounge about 66 ft. by 66 ft. by 11 ft. 4 high.
3504 – The oak flooring to centre of room, with teak border, about 66 ft. by 21 ft. (Titanic International Society, Joe Carvalho Collection; Alex Cheek Collection)

Next page: This is how the first-class Smoking Room (Lot 3512), perhaps one of the most beautiful rooms to put to sea, was described in the 1935 disbursal sale catalogue. *The finely carved mahogany panelling to room, with supporting pillars, and floral and scroll ornamentation and egg and tongue mouldings, inlaid mother-o'-pearl in scroll and floral designs as fixed throughout, having numerous leaded glass panels and windows, with scenic and figure panels, forming four bay windows, with leaded panels over, two side-screens with plate-glass panels, a three-sided screen, enclosing cloak room, chimney breast, with oil painting in panel over fireplace—"New York Harbour," by Norman Wilkinson, 31 in. by 68 in., the whole fitted two doors with plate-glass panels to aft companionway, two panelled doors to lavatories, door-frame to starboard verandah café, folding revolving door to port verandah café with brass and glazed panels on café side, the doors having plate-glass upper panels including the ormolu and brass door fittings complete, the floor springs to doors, the ormolu bell-presses and the pierced brass pipe coverings where fitted at floor level, also the moulded and painted panelled ceilings to bays, and the main ceiling in three sections, with raised mouldings, the reeded mahogany carvings to uprights and the mahogany carvings on ceiling, size of room: 64 ft. by 62 ft. 6 overall by 11 ft. 6 high.* (Titanic International Society, Joe Carvalho Collection)

Inset: This is how the room appeared when *Olympic* was in service and was taken from a similar angle as the previous photo. (J&C McCutcheon Collection)
Above: (Titanic International Society, Joe Carvalho Collection)

The aft port corner of the Smoking Room while *Olympic* was at Jarrow. To the left, the sliding mahogany panel and shelf below was the pantry's "bar pass through." In 1911, the concept of an American-style bar was unknown on British ocean liners. Rather than ordering a drink at a bar, the steward took the passenger's drink order and brought it to him.

The rectangle on the wall to the right of the door was a green baize notice board. The glass-topped cigar humidor which sat just beneath this notice board has already been removed along with all the other furniture and light fixtures. The revolving door led to the port Verandah Café.

Just out of view on the left was lot 3513: 'The sculptured veined marble mantlepiece, with floral cornucopia, shell ornamentations, egg and tongue borders, 8 ft. by 4. ft. 9, enclosing massive ornamental steel grate, with brass rampant lion terminals and trellis-pattern iron recess, also the veined marble hearth and kerb en suite.' One wonders where this massive decorative feature is today. (Titanic International Society, Joe Carvalho Collection)

Many changes were made to *Olympic*'s interiors over the course of her service life, but her classic Smoking Room only received a few updates. New linoleum tile flooring was installed after the wear and tear of the war years, and the chairs and sofas received new soft-leather coverings. Despite being over twenty-five years old, the paneling still glows. The door to the right leads to the steward's pantry and bar which was located just behind the fireplace. On the opposite side of the bulkhead in front of the cameraman was the starboard Verandah Café.

For many years, researchers had thought this room was lost. In November, 2003, however, part of the Smoking Room appeared on an on-line auction site. The start price was ridiculously high, and the paneling never sold despite numerous attempts over the years, but at least it is now known that some of the beautiful mahogany paneling exists. One has to wonder how much more of this lovely paneling (as well as other *Olympic* woodwork) survives in other private residences throughout the United Kingdom. (Titanic International Society, Joe Carvalho Collection)

The aft entrance to the second-class library during the strip-out at Jarrow. The beautiful sycamore paneling gleamed right up until the end. Oddly, the base of the aft mast came down only about four feet forward directly in front of this door, giving passengers very little space to enter or exit. Note the metal steam radiator grill at the bottom of the wall. The 1935 auction catalogue listed the room in two lots:

3819 The oak parquet flooring as laid, about 9 yards by 7 yards. [N.B. In the original catalogue, '9' and '7' were crossed out by hand and changed to '8' and '6' respectively.]
3820 The sycamore panelling with mahogany dado, twelve window frames, eight columns, three glazed panel doors, etc., about 222 ft. run, by 8 ft. high, twelve wooden curtain rods and fittings, twelve fringed rep pelmets, the painted wood ceiling, and seventy-eight electric ceiling lamps and roses.
(Titanic International Society, Joe Carvalho Collection)

Above left: This view, looking over the ship-breaking yard situated on the site of the old Palmers shipbuilding facility, gives a sense of the chaos. In this organized confusion, one of the best-loved liners of the twentieth century was reduced to bits. Cutting is far advanced now and just visible is what is left of the famous White Star yellow-gold sheer line above the double ports of D Deck.

The vast majority of the ship and her fittings were recycled for further use. Even unremarkable items like staircases, tile floors, urinals, etc., were given a new lease on life. It seems inconceivable these days that anyone would save such mundane items, but in the depths of the Depression, any high-quality item was put back into service. The ever-frugal Cunard White Star itself recycled some items from *Olympic*. For example, the carpet from her *à la carte* Restaurant was reused on board *Aquitania* in her Restaurant. Many of *Olympic*'s large silver pieces were sent to the *Queen Mary* when she entered service and used in the third-class Dining Room. Pieces remain on board to this day. Some of the items on the *Queen Mary*

can be traced directly back to the original service from *Olympic* because of the pattern and date markings. Other reusable White Star silver serving pieces went into Cunard storage, and some eventually found its way onto the *Queen Elizabeth 2*, a few pieces still being on board as late as the 1980s. (Ken Marschall Collection)

Above right: After the hull had been cut down to near the original waterline, on September 19, 1937, the remains of *Olympic*'s hull were towed to Inverkeithing for final demolition. As one newspaper said: 'She was the best hull to ever come out of Harland & Wolff.' Hanging askew off the port stern is the original warning sign that reads: 'This vessel has triple screws. Keep clear.'

Olympic's name was removed from British registry on February 4, 1939, with the note 'vessel broken up at Inverkeithing.' When the final section of *Olympic*'s double bottom was lifted out of the water and sent to the smelter, White Star's pre-war glory had come to an end. (Eric Sauder Collection)

CHAPTER 7

A TOUR OF *OLYMPIC*

Olympic arrived in New York on the same day her sister *Titanic* left Southampton on her maiden voyage, April 10, 1912. After the loss of *Titanic* on April 15, *Olympic* reached Southampton on the 21st. At the start of her next journey, however, part of her crew mutinied because of the perceived questionable quality of the newly installed collapsible boats. After numerous delays, *Olympic* finally sailed for New York on May 15, arriving on May 22, for the first time since the loss of *Titanic*.

On May 25, Michigan Senator William Alden Smith, Chairman of the US Senate Subcommittee investigating the sinking of *Titanic*, made a surprise visit to *Olympic* and toured her with an eye toward getting a better feeling for the ship and, in a sense, 'experiencing' *Titanic*. The following photographs were taken that day and showcase many locations that were important to the Inquiry. Considering the locations photographed – many of which were off limits to passengers – it is probable that these images were taken for the benefit of the Inquiry – given some of the locations photographed. As presented here, they have been laid out to resemble a walking tour of the liner from forecastle to fantail.

All photos in the color section are from the collection of LuxuryLinerRow.com unless otherwise noted.

Opposite: In this impressive image, one immediately notices the fine, uncluttered lines of the ship. The sheer (the fore-and-aft curvature of the liner) and the much larger hydraulically driven rivets starting just under the well deck are clearly visible. *Olympic* was constructed with heavier shell plating and more rivets in areas where she flexed more at sea.

Left: What *Titanic* historian (or anyone attracted to her compelling tragedy) wouldn't love to take a walking tour of *Olympic*, given her nearly identical resemblance to her ill-fated sister? The photographer seems to focus on areas that were key in the *Titanic* disaster a few weeks earlier. Exploring *Olympic* with *Titanic* in mind is something that would have been enlightening at any time, but this would have been especially true immediately following the sinking. *Olympic* underwent many changes throughout her service life, and by the end of her career, there were many areas that were unrecognizable from her original specifications.

Right: The double doors just to the right of the staircase leading up to the forecastle go down to third-class areas. Note that the crew is washing the deck. Maintenance has always been a constant issue at sea, and crews have to be meticulous in protecting the ship as best they can from the ravages of salt water and salty air.

Left: *Olympic*'s vast amount of deck space for first-class passengers was unprecedented. Shown here is the starboard promenade on A Deck looking aft. On B Deck below, a similar amount of deck space was available, but after *Olympic* entered service, White Star management realized that the promenade space on B Deck was little used and could be better utilized as revenue-earning deluxe cabins on her younger sister *Titanic*.

Right: One of the few known photos of the bridge on *Olympic*, which clearly shows the equipment. The telegraph on the far left was for the reciprocating engines, the middle telegraph was for docking instructions, and the one on the right was an emergency engine telegraph if the engine telegraph was disabled. The single, non-reversible turbine was disconnected from the power train when the ship was going slowly as it would be in most maneuvering situations; therefore, no telegraph was needed for the turbine.

The helm seen here was connected to the main wheel in the wheelhouse (just out of frame to the left). Behind the wheel is the binnacle (the non-magnetic housing for the ship's compass), and attached to the forward wall is a dark arch-shaped box which indicated the ship's course. The liner's storm windows are the dark objects with round openings stored below the windows, ready to be put up in rough weather.

91426

olympic

Above: The aft wall of *Olympic*'s wheelhouse was filled with important ship's equipment. Directly in front of the camera is a course indication board, which reminded the officer on watch of the correct course. The reflective round glass in the center is a barometer, and to the right, covered in cheese-cloth, is a clock. Given the night-vision sensitivity of the wheelhouse, it is interesting to note that the phone indicator lights under each telephone had small covers that could be closed to hide the light. One of these phones communicates with the crow's nest and is identical to that on *Titanic* on which Sixth Officer Moody was alerted to an 'iceberg right ahead' just over a month before this photo was taken.

Opposite: The only known image showing the starboard aft corner of the wheelhouse and the shelving which stored some of the lifeboat equipment and rations. Each lantern, hatchet, compass, etc., was fitted into a space that was marked with its boat number, and the large white boxes next to the lanterns contained hardtack and are watertight. This shelving unit and its mate on the port side are shown on *Olympic*'s general arrangement plans, and although *Titanic* was quite different in her wheelhouse layout, she no doubt had the same type of shelving. The shiny linoleum floor tiles are identical to those found in second- and third-class areas of the White Star trio and are also still on the floor of the wheelhouse on the wreck of *Britannic* in the Aegean.

Left: This remarkable image shows the third funnel. This set of triple-chime whistles (as well as the set of the fourth funnel) were dummies. Only the whistles on the first and second funnels were operational.

Opposite: An unusual view of the first-class staircase looking toward the aft port corner on Boat Deck. Although fortunate for us, one wonders why the photographer decided to take a picture looking aft instead of toward the lavish clock panel. This is the first time that a photo of the aft wall of the entrance gallery and its port vestibule and decorative carved oak garland has surfaced. The rug on the balcony is very interesting, as is the lack of chairs around the balustrade. This is our best view yet to show us how *Titanic*'s entrances were likely furnished.

Although difficult to see, the stair tread facings are no longer brass as they had been when the ship was new. At some point in *Olympic*'s first few months of service, the brass ones were replaced by rubber nosings. No one knows exactly when this was done, but given this photo, it is now certain that the nosings were changed long before her 1913 refit, as previously thought. Given that this photo was taken in May, 1912, it seems almost certain that *Titanic* had rubber nosings as well.

1427

Lifeboat drill on *Olympic*. Under the direction of the deck officer in the foreground, the crew is preparing Boat #10 for launching. The Berthon collapsible inboard of the lifeboat is being readied to be unfolded. What is unusual is that the officer is wearing a frock coat, which would normally be seen in a more formal setting and not in the performance of his regular deck duties, perhaps another indication of the importance of these photos. This scene is as close as one will ever get to seeing *Titanic*'s lifeboats being launched.

This view of the aft port lifeboats was taken from the roof of the liner's water tank room, a non-passenger area. Gravity was used to provide water pressure; therefore, the tanks were placed high up on Boat Deck. The photographer had to cart his bulky tripod, heavy camera, and glass-plate negatives up a vertical ladder to get on the deck house for this view.

Left: Taken at the aft end of Boat Deck looking forward, this view shows one of the Berthon collapsibles in its stowed position. The supposed frail nature of these boats was the instigation for the partial crew mutiny that delayed *Olympic*'s first sailing after *Titanic*'s loss the previous month.

Opposite: A view from the aft end of boat deck looking over the poop deck. The large wooden box to the left was a lifebelt locker. In an emergency, it was thought that passengers would not always be able to get back to their cabins for their life preservers; so extras were provided on deck. A large number of new collapsible boats have also been added to the fantail.

Opposite: Lifeboat No. 9. The photographer is standing on the engineer's promenade, the aft-most end of which is delineated by the railing seen in front of the Berthon collapsible on the right of the image. Aft of the railing is second class. Interestingly, the collapsible is in its open position.

Right: Taken from the forward end of the poop deck looking over the well deck, this view shows an interesting feature in the layout of the *Olympic* class. The uppermost deck was second class, which looked down onto first class. Note the crew member standing by the gate leading down to the well deck, which was a third-class area. The sign on the gate reads: 'Notice – 3rd Class Passengers are not Allowed on This Deck.' Even though the deck directly across from the photographer is a second-class area, several passengers from first class have come down for a look. In many instances, the class distinctions that permeated the ship while at sea were abandoned while in port.

This view is similar to what Quartermaster Rowe saw as *Titanic* struck the iceberg. At the time of the collision, he was on the poop deck and 'felt a slight jar, and I looked at my watch. It was … twenty minutes to twelve. I looked toward the starboard side of the ship and saw a mass of ice … It was very close to the ship, almost touching it.'

Opposite: Looking forward from the aft docking bridge.

Right: Having disembarked, the photographer took this picture of the starboard bow, perhaps trying to show the general area on *Titanic* where the iceberg struck. Canvas has been rigged on the forward end of the A Deck promenade to help prevent strong winds from blowing down the deck. Because her A Deck open promenade was never enclosed, these canvas screens show up throughout her life.

Opposite page: Now our cameraman has moved upriver to Pier 60. As the size of liners increased, the piers in Manhattan had to be extended into the river to accommodate the new giants. The extension on which the photographer is standing was added to accommodate the new White Star trio.

The ends of the aft docking bridge on *Olympic* were flush with the liner's side. The teak grate standing vertically at the edge of the docking bridge, seen in close-up on the inset photo, could be lowered as needed and allowed the officer on duty a better view below while docking. Gratings like these were not necessary on *Titanic* because the docking bridge itself was extended over the side of the liner.

Off *Olympic*'s stern in the distance is the French liner *Rochambeau*.

Right: One final view as the great liner departs Pier 59 for another trip home.

WHITE STAR STEAMER "OLYMPIC," 46,439 TONS.

THE WHITE STAR LINER R.M.S. "OLYMPIC" — LENGTH 882 FEET BEAM 92 FEET, DEPTH (FROM KEEL TO BOAT DECK) 97 FEET, A

A rare full-color cutaway issued by White Star in about 1920. Note that she has been converted to burn oil. (Brian Hawley Collection)

Left: A not-often-seen color view of the second-class Dining Room. (Brian Hawley Collection)

439, SPEED 22½ KNOTS. IN EQUIPMENT IT IS UNSURPASSED BY ANYTHING AFLOAT, AS CAN BE SEEN FROM THE DIAGRAMATIC PICTURE OF ITS INTERIOR.

Right: A very rare color view of the third-class Smoking Room. (Brian Hawley Collection)

Olympic's enduring popularity lives on today in the world of ocean-liner memorabilia. Her in-service china and silver, in particular, are extremely popular and are quickly purchased by collectors. These beautiful pieces are all from her first-class service, and nearly all date to her maiden voyage in 1911. (Brian Hawley Collection)

In the days before World War I, when there were no gift shops on board the liners, the ship's barber was in charge of selling souvenirs, such as this spoon, toothpick pot, and lapel pin. The pin continues to cross the Atlantic to this day and has been worn by the author on numerous crossings. Also seen is an officer's brass uniform button, and the model of *Olympic* is a paperweight made from her brass by Thomas Ward, the firm that scrapped her. (Brian Hawley Collection)

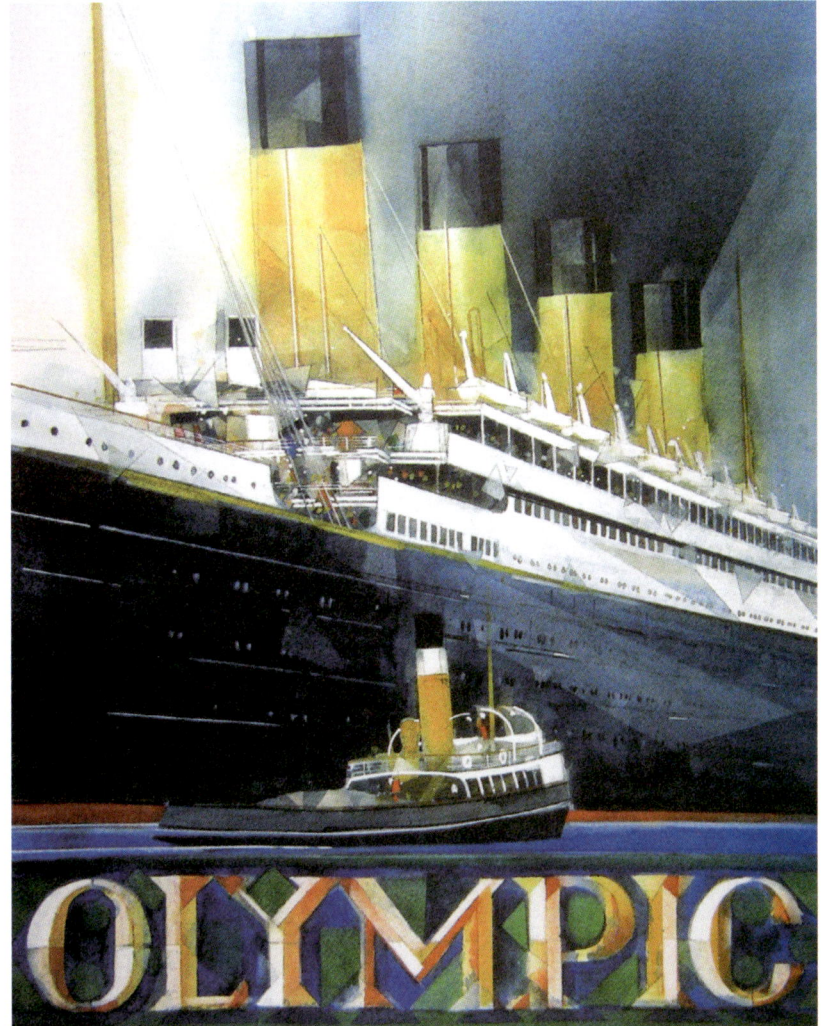

A lovely painting by Don Stoltenburg, showing his unique style applied to great effect. (From an original painting by Don Stoltenburg.)

This and opposite page: Two superb paintings by Capt. Stephen Card depicting *Olympic* in Southampton water – one of her flying the White Star flag; the other showing her under the double house flags of the newly merged Cunard White Star. Both paintings are currently on display on board Cunard's *Queen Mary 2*. (From original oil paintings by Stephen J. Card, A.F.N.I.)

WHITE STAR LINE
R.M.S. "OLYMPIC",

BOAT DECK

DECK "A"

DECK "B"

DECK "C"

EMERGENCY B STATION

EMERGENCY B STATION

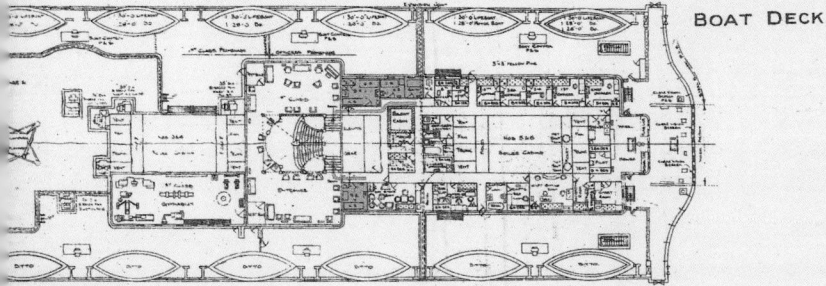

Plan Showing Position of Emergency Stations and Routes.

Passengers should follow the routes shown by the Arrows tinted similarly to the colour of their accommodation as indicated on this plan.

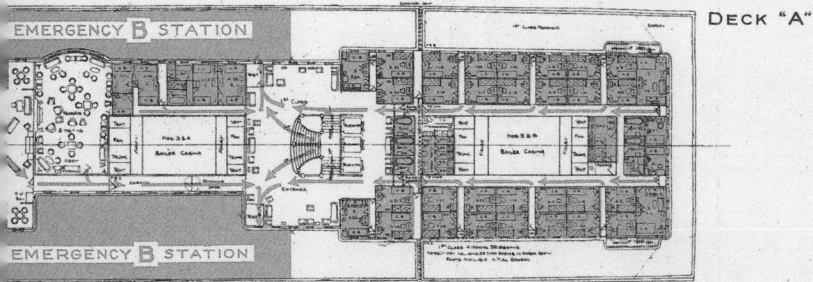

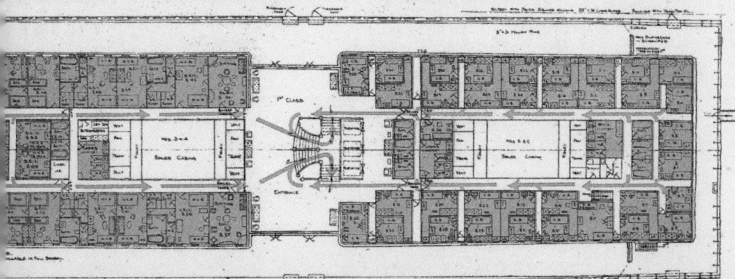

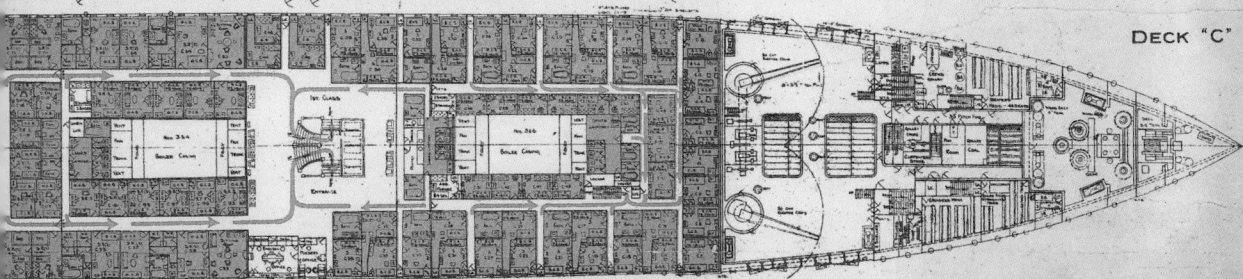

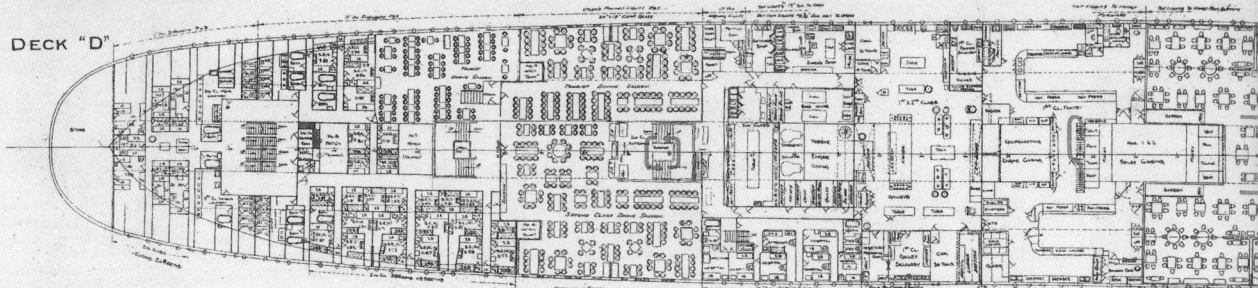

DECK "D"

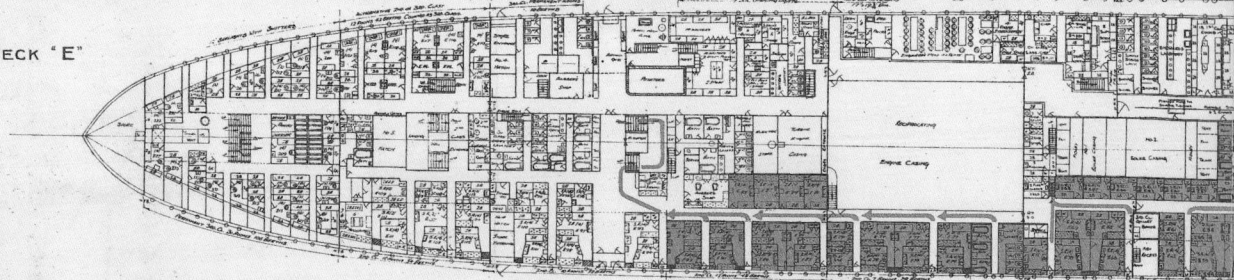

DECK "E"

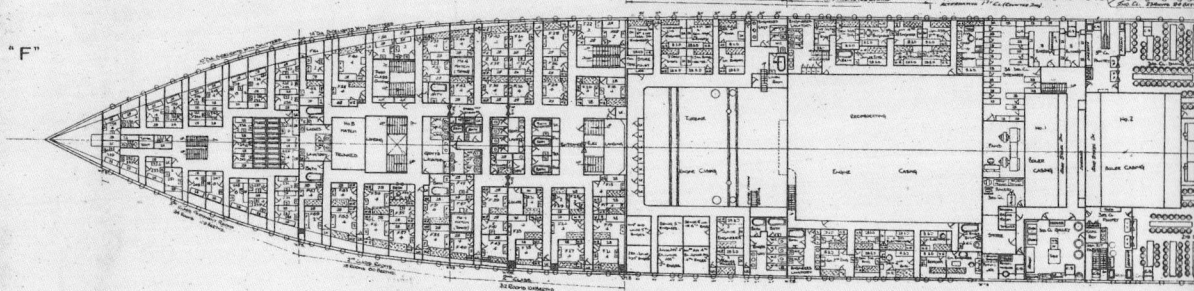

DECK "F"

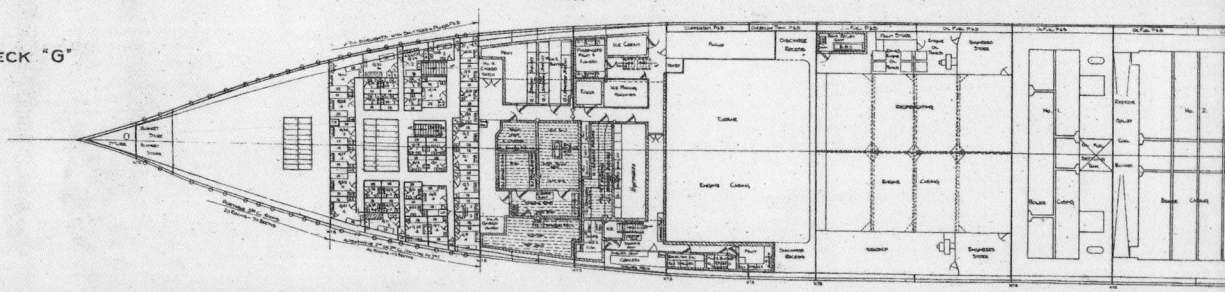

DECK "G"

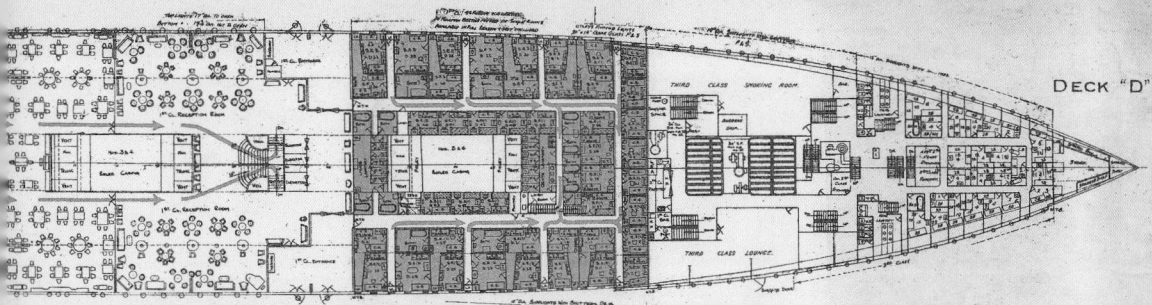

DECK "D"

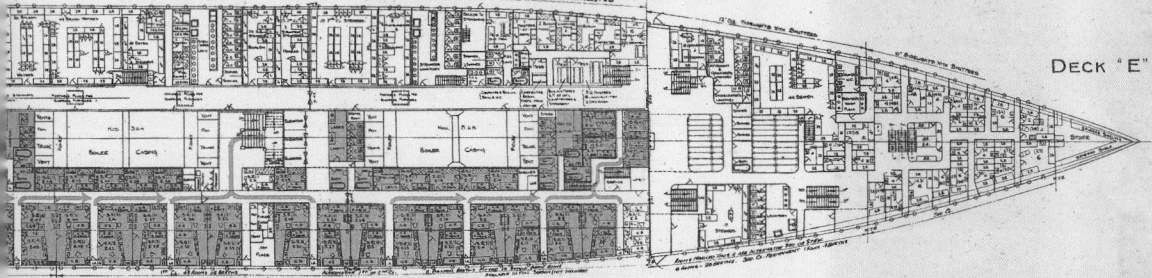

DECK "E"

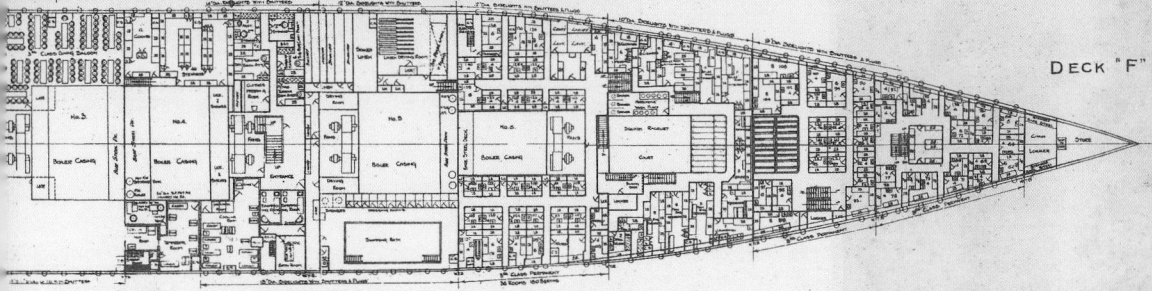

DECK "F"

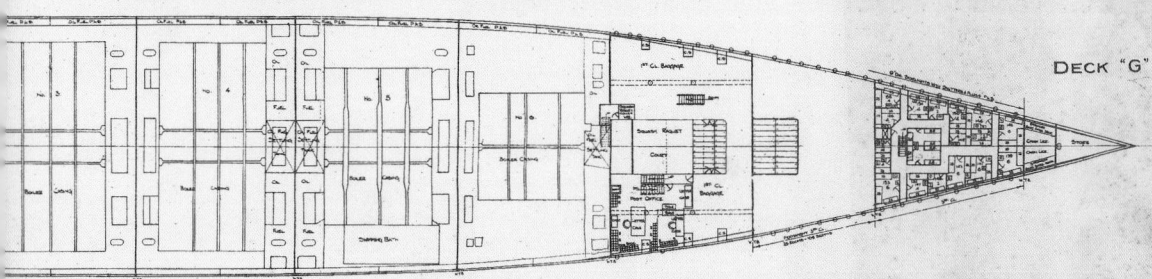

DECK "G"

BIBLIOGRAPHY

Anderson, Roy, *White Star*, T. Stephenson & Sons, 1964

Beaumont, J.C.H., *Ships and People*, Geoffrey Bles, Suffolk St., Pall Mall, London, 1930

Bonsall, Thomas E., *Titanic*, Gallery Books, 1987

Braynard, Frank O., *Leviathan*, Six Volumes, South Street Seaport Museum, 1972

Braynard, Frank O. and William H. Miller, *Fifty Famous Liners*, W.W. Norton and Co., Inc., 1985

Chirnside, Mark, *RMS Olympic: Titanic's Sister*, Tempus Publishing, Ltd., 2004

Chirnside, Mark, *The Olympic-Class Ships: Olympic, Titanic, and Britannic*, Tempus Publishing, 2004

DeKerbrech, Richard, *Ships of the White Star Line*, Ian Allan Publishing, 2006

Dempsey, John, *I've Seen Them All Naked*, Waterfront Publications, 1992

Eaton, John P. & Charles A. Haas, *Falling Star*, W.W. Norton & Co., 1990

Green, Edwin & Michael Moss, *A Business of National Importance*, Methuen & Co., Ltd., 1982

Hayes, Bertram Sir, *Hull Down*, The Macmillan Company, 1925

Hutchings, David F., *RMS Titanic: A Modern Legend*, Waterfront Publications, 1993

Hyde, Francis E., *Cunard and the North Atlantic 1840-1973*, The Macmillan Press, Ltd., 1975

Kludas, Arnold, *Great Passenger Ships of the World*, 5 Volumes., Patrick Stephens, Ltd., 1972-1976

Maxtone-Graham, John, *The Only Way to Cross*, The Macmillan Company, 1972

Maxtone-Graham, John, *Epilogue to Olympic & Titanic: Ocean Liners of the Past*, Patrick Stephens, 1983

Maxtone-Graham, John, *Cunard: 150 Glorious Years*, David & Charles, 1989

McCart, Neil, *Atlantic Liners of the Cunard Line*, Thorsons Publishers, 1990

Mills, Simon, *RMS Olympic: The Old Reliable*, Waterfront Publications, 1993

Mylon, Patrick, *The White Star Collection: A Shipping Line in Postcards*, The History Press, 2011

Oldham, Wilton J., *The Ismay Line*, The Journal of Commerce, 1961

Parker, Captain, Walter H., *Leaves from an Unwritten Log-book*, Sampson Low, Marston & Co., 1931

Warren, Mark D., *The Shipbuilder, 1906-1914*, Volume 1, Blue Riband Publications, Inc., 1995

Warren, Mark D., *The Shipbuilder, 1907-1914*, Volume 2, Blue Riband Publications, Inc., 1997